CHINA DIARIES

& OTHER TALES FROM THE ROAD

JOHN H. RYDZEWSKI

INKWATER
PRESS

*Scan this QR Code
to learn more about
this title*

Publisher: Inkwater Press | www.inkwaterpress.com

Paperback
ISBN-13 978-1-59299-834-0 | ISBN-10 1-59299-834-8

Kindle
ISBN-13 978-1-59299-835-7 | ISBN-10 1-59299-835-6

ePub
ISBN-13 978-1-59299-836-4 | ISBN-10 1-59299-836-4

Printed in the U.S.A.
All paper is acid free and meets all ANSI standards for archival quality paper.

1 3 5 7 9 10 8 6 4 2

*To my Mother for all her love, patience
and understanding as I explored the world;
and to my uncle, Joe Rinke, who inspired
me to travel long before I stepped onto my
first airplane, but with whom I never had
a chance to trade road-warrior stories.*

CONTENTS

FOREWORD

CHINA. JUST THE MENTION OF THE PLACE ELICITS A WIDE VARIETY OF unsolicited opinions about the country, its politics and its people, mostly from those who learned about China from what the TV and the newspapers told them. In 2006 when I told my friends and family I committed to a two-year job assignment in China as an expatriate (expat) even though I didn't yet know the city in China where I would be living, some of them too provided me with plenty of unsolicited opinions about my mental condition. But by the time I broke this news to them, I had been back and forth to China about a half dozen times since 2003, and knew enough Mandarin to direct a cabbie, order a beer, and to negotiate prices in the markets. I realized that what they thought they knew about China and what I saw in China with my very own eyes were two completely different universes.

My transition from the U.S. to China happened from September 2006 through January 2007 and came in the form of whirlwind travel between the U.S., various places in Europe, and at least two weeks each month in Shànghǎi. It was five months of continuous jet-lag, but I believe that the sense of freedom induced from my ultra-mobile lifestyle – and the prospect of starting a brand-new job where creativity was encouraged – gave me the inspiration to resurrect in earnest my writing hobby that had otherwise took a backseat to the daily grind of working in corporate America. As I traveled from place to place, ideas began to form into stories, and from there I would send off an email to a few close friends. By December 2006, during some downtime over the Christmas holiday, I decided that instead of pelting my friends with email, it was time to start a blog with previous and new stories that people could check at their own leisure. I used the blog format to post stories and photos to help educate and entertain my friends, family, and random strangers surfing the internet about what I saw on the ground in China and during my travels. I started my foreign assignment in Shànghǎi (上海) in January 2007, moved to Dàlián (大连), China, on September 1, 2007, and stayed until May 1, 2010. Most of this book was written while I was living in Dalian.

It was more than just inspiration that turned me back on to writing. Each time I entered China for a visit, I felt as though a transition was occurring within my neural network. My brain had to adapt to the multitude of sensory inputs, process them, and then put every piece of the puzzle into its proper place as it tried to make sense of everything and everybody I encountered. I swore I could feel the neurons in my brain reconfigure themselves into new networks to help me understand what I was seeing, hearing, smelling, and tasting. Maybe it was just my imagination that I could feel the neurons growing, but China had brought to me a new sense of enlightenment. From this enlightenment and a desire to learn about China and Asia, I became a knowledge sponge: besides my full-time day job, I attended six hours per week of one-on-one Chinese lessons, and studied those lessons for hours outside of class; set off on numerous travel excursions around the country; kept up with social engagements; made a point to hit the gym a few times a week; and still found time to write. Looking back, I realized that I was in my groove, and found the sweet spot where I was able to make the most of every opportunity. There's

no doubt I was undergoing a fundamental change that would eventually become deep and permanent.

When I realized that I was getting ready to ride the crest of
a huge wave of creativity, I promised myself that I would write
a 2,000-word blog post on one specific subject per month for
every month I was in China, but if I wasn't inspired to write,
then I wouldn't. That is, all the stories had to flow naturally from
thought, through fingers and keyboard, and onto the screen. Soon
after posting one story, I would draw from my pipeline of story
ideas and start making observations for the next. This happened
just about every month with the exception of a couple, and then I
broke my promise and made myself write a story when I wasn't
inspired. But after a friend dropped me a note to tell me that he
thought a story (not included in this book) was "forced" because it
wasn't like the others, I no longer pressured myself to write. From
then on, like water down a hill, or the morning after an ultra-
spicy Sìchuān (四川) dinner, all my stories had to flow naturally.
One story — Flat Stanley — flowed almost too naturally, and after
I posted it a few friends wrote to me to express more concerns
about the effect China was having on me and asked me whether it
was time for me to return to the U.S.

Writing was not only a way for me to educate and entertain my
friends and family who questioned my whole Chinese adventure,
but the writing process itself — observing the people and places
around me, asking many questions, and finding patterns and asso-
ciations between them — helped me to learn more about China,
the people, the language, and the culture. Whenever I was in a car
going from one place to another, be it in a taxi or with my own
car and driver[1], I would always look out the windows to see what

1   For insurance and liability reasons, each foreign expat was provided with a car
    and a personal driver who would take us wherever we wanted to go. Drivers were
    assigned to their foreign charges at the start of their assignment, and if all worked
    out, they remained with the foreigner until the end of the assignment. I had no
    desire to drive in China.

people were doing, where they were going, how they were doing it, how they were dressed, and then wonder why they were doing it, how they earned their money, and so on. If I passed a village, I observed the houses, how they were built, and then wondered about their overall architecture, how many people lived there, how long they had lived there, what their future would be, etc. I would then tell my Chinese friends what I saw and heard, and would then ask them to explain it to me in more detail. In a couple instances, when driving through the Chinese countryside with a half-dozen other people on a business trip, I'd request that our van pull over – to the dismay of the others, I'm sure, but there's something to be said for being "the foreigner" – so I could get out to take a closer look at something or to take a photo rather than it being a blur along the highway. It was almost like being a kid again, learning and seeing new things for the very first time and then wanting to tell everyone about what I saw.

Because of my Zen-like approach to writing by writing only when inspired to do so, my blog – and, in some respects, this book – turned into a compilation of random experiences and thoughts, mostly based on my time living, working, and traveling China. When I headed to other countries such as Laos, Vietnam, Cambodia, Korea, Myanmar, Fiji, the Philippines, and New Zealand, I would bring with me a journal to scratch down some thoughts in the event a story bubbled up from deep down inside. Sometimes they did, and sometimes they didn't. And sometimes my predictions came true. I take special pride in writing in February 2010 that the U.S. would begin to normalize economic and diplomatic relations with Myanmar, which it did in January 2012. Other times, when I traveled in and out of China for vacations and business trips, if something hit me, I would be compelled to write about it, then and there, in real time (David M., the TSA Officer in Syracuse, New York; my Zurich, Switzerland airport hotel) because I knew I had to harness that creativity and inspiration before it left me forever.

When I returned to the U.S. in May 2010, the inspiration to write new material left me just as suddenly as it came. I wrote one last story about my repatriation back to Portland, Oregon – the last chapter of this book – but soon after that, it was as if someone turned off the tap and my thoughts and ideas stopped flowing. This just went to show how precious and fleeting creative inspiration can be. But all was not lost. I discontinued posting new material to my blog, closed down the website, and decided to focus my efforts on turning my best and favorite blog posts into stories for this travel book. I can only hope that this book will be as entertaining for you to read as it was for me to write, and that it will provide you with new insights and different perspectives about China and Asia; and give you inspiration to further explore the world in which we live.

Many names have been omitted or truncated to protect both the innocent and the guilty.

CHAPTER 1

HIGHWAYS OF DEATH

FOR THE TWO AND A HALF YEARS WÁNG (王) WAS MY DRIVER IN Dàlián, I had a difficult time getting him to wear his seatbelt. Mind you, he wouldn't wear his seatbelt but he stashed two bulletproof vests in the trunk of our black VW Passat even though it was against the law for private citizens to own firearms. After a while, I pretty much left it up to him whether or not he wanted to fasten his seatbelt. Then one day, he started wearing it without any prompting. I'm sure it had everything to do with the woman he saw fly through her windshield during a head-on collision during his lunch break. At the time, the traffic fine for not wearing a seatbelt was 50 RMB[1] ($7.25) per violation, but Wáng thought the woman paid a much higher price. So went another typical day on China's highways of death.

The Chinese don't like seatbelts of any kind, whether in automobiles or airplanes. This was evident on a flight from Shànghǎi to Dàlián when I had the awkward task of helping a cute but married Chinese woman next to me fasten her belt low and tight

---

1   The Chinese currency is formally referred to as the *Yuán* (元), but it is also known in China as the *Rénmínbì* (人民币), or "People's Money", abbreviated as RMB. The *Yuán* and *Rénmínbì* are equivalent. RMB is used as the standard abbreviation throughout this book.

around her tiny little waist; or in downtown Dàlián where I saw a car with the telltale and very painful head print in the passenger's side of the windshield. During one morning commute, we passed a truck that rear-ended a car, saw that the windshield of the truck was blown out, and the driver was no longer behind the wheel. People seem to be oblivious to the fact that driving is like sky-diving: it's not the speed that kills, but the sudden stop.

My 20-mile commute to the office was mostly on a three-lane highway buzzing with cars, buses, trucks, bicycles, mopeds, pedestrians, you name it. On an average day in Dàlián, I saw two or three traffic accidents. On one particularly bad day, I saw eight. In my first few months I saw well over 200 traffic accidents. Most were fender-benders, but once in a while I passed a real mess. Every other month or so, I watched blood flow red on the highway as the injured, sprawled out on the road and surrounded by spectators, waited for help to arrive. Some were beyond help.

On one dark winter morning I saw several people standing over a body lying in an intersection, lit up only by the headlights of a police car. At dinner one night I asked ten expat friends whether or not they had seen dead bodies in the road. All ten said "yes", and some had seen bodies multiple times. Apparently only expats saw human roadkill because none of my Chinese friends ever admitted to seeing any, and were in disbelief when I told them about the dead people.

In some ways, there are financial incentives for killing those who would otherwise be merely injured in a car accident. According to my Chinese friends who drive, drivers who hit someone become responsible for the victim's medical bills and lost wages. Depending on who is hit and how badly, this can become a very expensive proposition. During the Great Recession of 2008, word on the street was that some of the unemployed were carefully stepping in front of passing cars in hopes of cashing in on a free ride. In February 2012, a non-Chinese friend of mine who drives a Mercedes in Dàlián said to me that he would occasionally see pedestrians apparently weighing the pros and cons of stepping out in front of him just for the payout. So, as all the Chinese drivers know, if they are going to hit pedestrians, then they should hit 'em hard because the lump sum for a fatality can be significantly less expensive than if the victim survived. In October 2011, a 2-year-old girl was run over three times in less than ten minutes while bystanders looked on and did nothing. The man who first struck the girl with his front tire, paused, and then rolled over her again with his rear tire, said to the Chinese media, "If she is dead, I may pay only about 20,000 yuan ($3,125 [at the time]). But if she is injured, it may cost me hundreds of thousands of yuan." The girl later died at a hospital.[2] Then there are those who go above and beyond, such as Yào Jiāxīn (药家鑫), the 21-year-old, third-year student at the Xī'ān Conservatory of Music, who on October 10,

---

2   http://www.thetruthaboutcars.com/2011/10/
     watch-a-child-run-over-three-times-or-don%E2%80%99t/

2010, after clipping and causing minor injuries to Zhāng Miào (张妙) – a 26-year-old mother of two who was riding her bicycle – stopped and stabbed her to death so she wouldn't call the police to report the accident. Yào was later apprehended after causing a second accident while fleeing the murder. He was sentenced to death in April 2011 and executed on June 7, 2011.

Further incentivizing the wrong driving behaviors is the Chinese definition of "right of way". When I first moved to Dàlián I was told that if a driver was turning onto a road and didn't look to see if other cars were coming, then the driver of the car that hits the turning car was responsible for the accident because they didn't take action to avoid the car that pulled out in front of them. But if the driver who pulled onto a main road looked both ways before being hit by the oncoming traffic, then the driver who pulled into traffic is responsible for the accident because he knew he was about to cause one. So, Chinese drivers pull out into traffic willy-nilly without looking both ways before they turn, lest they be required to pay for the damage caused by an accident.

Hú, Wēn, Baker, and Baker, in their 2008 study[3] entitled "Road-Traffic Deaths in China, 1985-2005: Threat and Opportunity", calculated that the rate of traffic deaths in China increased by 100 percent over those twenty years and that traffic injuries were the leading cause of death of Chinese people less than 45 years of age. In a September 2010 study[4] for the World Health Organization, Hú, Baker and Baker showed that the Chinese police significantly underestimated the number of traffic deaths, including those in 2000 when the Chinese police celebrated a milestone when traffic deaths for the first time fell below 100,000 (81,649 vs. 221,135). Through statistical analysis they demon-

---

3   *Inj. Prev.* 2008 Jun; 14(3): 149-153.
4   Hú, G., Baker, T., and Baker, S.P., "Comparing Road Traffic Mortality Rates from Police-Reported Data and Death Registration Data in China", *Bulletin of the World Health Organization* 2011; 89:41-45. doi: 10.2471/BLT.10.080317, http://www. who.int/bulletin/volumes/89/1/10-080317/en/

strated that while police-reported traffic fatalities were showing a steady decline since 2002, the national death registration data showed a steady increase in traffic deaths since 2005.

Curiously, in their 2008 study, Hú, Wēn, Baker, and Baker found that regions with fewer people had the highest rates of traffic fatalities. While the authors blamed the rural deaths on poor road conditions, one could argue that the relatively empty roads in the Chinese countryside are faster roads traversed by less experienced drivers. My most harrowing driving experience in China occurred in a March 2005 goat-, people-, cow-, tractor- and truck-dodging road rally 80-90 mph on the two-lane roads in rural Héběi (河北) Province between the cities of Shíjiāzhuāng (石家庄) and Héngshuǐ (衡水). Taking second place was the two-hour crater-and-coal-truck dodging drive in April 2008 in Shānxī (山西) Province between town of Píngyáo (平遥) and the city of Tàiyuán (太原).

The number of traffic deaths may also be higher in rural and newly-developed urban areas because of people's attitudes toward the new roads. The analogy that comes to mind is a new American suburban development where, to the dismay of the new home owners, the deer and rabbits wander through the back-yards and eat the vegetable and flower gardens. Of course, the deer and rabbits were there before the homes, so they are going to continue their way of life even though some new buildings and streets showed up. The nice gardens just make it a little bit easier for them to forage. Similarly, the Chinese seem completely oblivious to the speeding traffic as they go about their normal business because a newly-opened, eight-lane highway that cuts through a neighborhood is more convenient to walk across than a muddy path or an out-of-the-way overpass. During my commute to work one morning, I saw a father, mother, and a one-year-old in his father's arms, standing on the median, halfway through their game of Frogger across six lanes speeding traffic and trying to figure out how to make it to the next level. It was common to see workers, with their tools in hand, bicycling or walking to work only a few inches away from speeding trucks that could, in an instant, turn them into a greasy spot; motorcycles and mopeds zipping the wrong way down the highway; and cars using the entrance ramp as an exit. This all gave a new definition to the word "freeway". I regularly saw people, as part of their daily commute, dashing out into the highways the same way deer do in rural upstate New York, where it makes better sense to watch the sides of the road rather than look straight ahead when driving. But like the deer in New York, not all the people make it across Chinese roads: Wáng and I were once stuck in a traffic jam while heading north out of town. As we crawled our way to the scene of the accident, all we saw was some scattered broken glass and an empty pair of matching shoes.

The Chinese freeways tended to be dangerous, but surface street intersections are, as the military boys like to say, "target-rich environments." It was common in Dàlián to see tractor trailers, buses, cars, and fully-loaded cement trucks ignore traffic lights. On many occasions, the only car that stopped for a red light was the one in which I was sitting because I told Wáng that he would be fired on the spot if he ever ran a red light. After seeing several accidents at one particular intersection near my office, I started calling it "The Intersection of Death".

Besides standard, run-of-the-mill, intersections, the Chinese have also taken a liking to traffic circles, which tend to be more like wheels of fortune than traffic control devices. While in the town of Zhōngdiàn (中甸) in Yúnnán (云南) Province in November 2010, my taxi driver went the wrong way around a traffic circle for three-quarters of a rotation when he could have simply bore to the right to make a legal turn. There are no real barriers — hard or administrative — preventing cars from going more than one direction on any road. On one evening in downtown Dàlián, I saw a guy drive the wrong way up a four-lane, one-way street at a relatively high rate of speed while the right-of-way traffic was also traveling toward him at about the same rate. The wrong way car passed a police car going in the correct direction and then cut across three lanes of traffic to make a left turn, but the cop the apparently couldn't be bothered and didn't take any action. Of course, after I saw another cop car on another day bust out a similar wrong-way move I realized my expectations for Chinese traffic law enforcement were set too high.

Law enforcement has a book of traffic laws to reference, but the only law that governs Chinese traffic is the Law of Gross Tonnage.[5] The Chinese high-octane approach to land-based navigation is taken to an entirely new level because ships and boats don't cruise at 100 miles per hour. Bus and truck drivers, rather than using their brakes when the vehicle in front of them begins to slow, swerve from lane to lane, honking their horns as they push forward. Once the big vehicle swerves, all smaller vehicles take action to prevent bad things from happening. It's when two big vehicles meet up that things could get real messy. During one drive home, I saw a cement truck at a high rate of speed blow through a red light and almost T-bone a bus filled with some very wide-eyed commuters. For whatever reason, drivers are hell-bent on getting from Point A to Point B even if people could die in the process. Further complicating my daily commute was when the gross tonnage in the form sand, gravel, dirt, and coal spilled out of the overloaded trucks and turned into death from above. Then again, if the loads were covered, the street sweepers – women braving highway traffic every morning with only a fluorescent orange jacket and a long-handled homemade broom of sticks and twigs – would lose their steady jobs that paid 20 RMB ($3.00 at the time) per day.

What is the reason for the behaviors and carnage on the Chinese roads? The published version of the Chinese traffic law looks just like that seen in the U.S. and elsewhere. But if the Chinese

---

5   The Law of Gross Tonnage is a nautical principal where the largest/heaviest boats and ships have right of way over smaller vessels.

traffic law is not much different than the western traffic laws, why are the Chinese roads the leading cause of death of those under 45? Like many major issues in China today – including the environmental pollution and poor water quality – it becomes a matter of enforcement. Enforcement requires money, which forces the setting of priorities. One could argue that higher fines would provide the revenue to develop a robust infrastructure of enforcement, but this still relies on grassroots enforcers to ensure the revenue makes it to its proper destination without it vaporizing along the shoulder of the highway. In the grand scheme of things, I think there are bigger fish to fry in China than to make sure everyone comes to a complete stop at stop signs, or uses their turn signals before turning. Maintaining social stability comes to mind. Hmmm...social stability or orderly traffic? I'd pick social stability, too, even though one could argue that orderly traffic will eventually lead to social stability. The study by Hú, Wēn, Baker, and Baker is a good effort that will eventually add benefit to Chinese society, but it seems a bit premature given China's current state of affairs. Then again, one could look at China's highway fatalities as an example of social engineering through Darwinism. If all plays out per the theories, the society will become smarter and stronger as it weeds itself out. With a population of 1.34 billion people, I don't see anyone in a big rush to stop the weeding...

On one particularly warm Spring day after work, one of those days when Mother Nature reassures everyone that winter had truly ended for another year, it was only fitting to see a young Chinese couple out for an early evening bike ride...and completely occupying the right lane of a three-lane freeway. Oblivious to the speeding cars, trucks and buses swerving around behind them, they chatted as they pedaled along. The gentleman was riding along the barricade while the girl was in the middle of traffic. It's really anyone's guess if either or both of them survived yet another typical day on China's highways of death.

CHAPTER 2

DESTINATION: DÀLIÁN

WHEN I FIRST COMMITTED MYSELF TO A TWO-YEAR JOB ASSIGNMENT IN China, I did not know where I'd be living. Location was secondary, or farther down the list. I was winging it and hoping for the best. After numerous vacation and business trips to China, all I knew was that I wanted to live and work in China, and the closer that I could get to the "real China" the happier I would be. That was the plan. The rest — where to live, the whole driver thing, whether or not I would have a job waiting for me when I returned to the U.S., etc. — were just details that I'd eventually figure out along the way.

Then came the day I was told that I'd be moving to Dàlián, China, considered by the *China Daily*, China's official English-language newspaper, as the Pearl of Northeast China.[6] Where? Get a map of China, and put your finger on Běijīng (北京). Now drag your finger to the east across the bay. Dàlián is the piece of Liáoníng (辽宁) Province that juts out into the Yellow Sea. If you get to North Korea, you've gone too far, but not that far since it's just a three-hour drive from Dàlián to the North Korean border. When I was in the eighth grade and learning about how

6   http://dalian.chinadaily.com.cn/2010-05/11/content_9818537.htm

the Japanese invaded Manchuria at the start of World War II, I never thought there would come a day when I would live a couple blocks from what was once the Japanese Imperial headquarters for Manchuria, better known today as Dàlián City Hall.

In September 2006, after the first full day of my maiden voyage to Dàlián with three of my coworkers, I started to ponder my next couple years. It was more apprehension than doubt now that the grand expectations of my Chinese assignment rammed head on into the reality of the situation. As we were quietly sipping our drinks at the Paulaner Bar in the basement of the Kempinski Hotel, I pictured myself sitting on the floor of my dark, empty Dàlián apartment on a frigid winter night, my back up against the concrete wall and a half-empty bottle of scotch between my legs, wondering what the hell I got myself into. It was then that I realized there was no turning back without a complete loss of credibility back home at the Mothership which honored my request to send me to China. There was no option except to push forward to the end and hope for the best. It was time for me to face the fact that I was given exactly what I wished for, and that I would have to make the most of it.

One year after that night at the Paulaner, I moved to Dàlián, home to about 5.4 million people.[7] Unlike the Tier 1 cities of Shànghǎi, Běijīng, and Guǎngzhōu (广州) that have been globalized, have living standards on par with other major cities in the world, and have Western expat populations in the tens of thousands, the Western expat population of Dàlián — a smaller and lesser-known Tier 2 city less tainted by globalization and Western influences — was in the hundreds. Not hundreds of thousands. Just the hundreds. An American friend who worked closely with the Dàlián police told me in October 2007 that Dàlián had around 200 legally registered Western households.

The literal English translation of "Dà Lián" is "big connect", which seems apt given the role ocean-based industry plays in connecting the local economy to the rest of the world. On the water's edge in downtown Dàlián is the Dàlián Shipbuilding Industry Company (DSIC), China's largest shipbuilding company and shipyard that began cranking out ships as a Russian company in 1898. DSIC and its 150,000 employees have perfected the art of shipbuilding: an American friend of mine who worked on the docks told me that, prior to the Great Recession, he watched DSIC launch, on average, one complete ocean freighter each month.

That connectedness took on an entirely new dimension during September 6-8 2007, when the World Economic Forum hosted its first "Summer Davos" conference there. Dàlián is hardly a quaint Swiss village, but the fact that the conference attracted the likes of *The World is Flat* author Thomas L. Friedman; HRM Queen Rania Al Abdullah of the Hashemite Kingdom of Jordan; Takashi Tsutsui, then CEO of the JASDAQ Securities Exchange

---

7   http://www.dalian-gov.net

in Tokyo; James J. Schiro, then Group CEO and Chairman of the Group Management Board of Zurich Financial in Zurich, Switzerland; Mohammed Al Gergaw, then Minister of State for Cabinet Affairs of the United Arab Emirates and Executive Chair of Dubai Holding; Anand P. Raman, then Senior Editor of the Harvard Business Review; and Craig Barrett, then Chairman of the Board of Intel Corporation, says something about where Dàlián is headed. Super-investor and billionaire Warren Buffett wasn't at the event, but he made a quick visit to Dàlián in October 2007 to check out one of his investments. Dàlián is also changing how it's connected to the rest of the world as it shifts from rustbelt industries to the internet. The Dàlián Software Park (大连软件园), established in 1998, houses companies such as IBM, HP, Accenture, Dell, Panasonic, Sony, Hitachi, NTT, Oracle, AVAYA, NEC, Cisco, plus a variety of Indian, Chinese, and Japanese ventures.

Business climate aside, Dàlián is most famous throughout China for its seafood, clean environment, and temperate weather. Even with millions of people, the city felt downright cozy when compared to some of China's other cities, and there are trees, green grass, and even a few hiking trails. When I made small talk with Chinese in other parts of the country, their first reaction to Dàlián was, "Dàlián is very beautiful!" so often that I could predict their reaction before I finished telling someone I lived there. Because everyone was so enthusiastic with their answer, it became natural to ask them how many times they had visited; only to find out that none had ever done so. By the same token, one Dàlián native told me that Dàlián was becoming a popular retirement destination among the wealthy Chinese, which is probably why the cost of living in this Tier 2 city was more comparable to Shànghǎi than it was to its Tier 2 sisters.

Dàlián also seemed to be a stepping stone to retirement for many Japanese businessmen whose companies are getting ready to put them to pasture. Although just about every Chinese citizen I talked with in my three and a half years in China privately acknowledged their hatred toward the Japanese, Dàlián is a popular outsourcing destination for dozens of Japanese companies (there are multiple daily flights between Dàlián and Osaka and Tokyo) staffed with ageing salarymen. In the evening hours, it's not uncommon to sit in one of the dozens of Japanese restaurants in the city and be surrounded by chain-smoking Japanese grandfathers paired up with 20-something Chinese cuties dolled-up to the nines. But with Dàlián and its hundreds of Japanese-only massage parlors, bars, and nightclubs, all at a fraction of the cost back home, what better place to be put to pasture? Word on the street had it that some Japanese bars in Dàlián accepted only Japanese Yen. A couple of American friends and I tried one night to enter such a Japanese club to see for ourselves, but the no-necked Chinese guy guarding the door — who was just as tall as he was wide — put a quick end to that idea.

Maybe Oddjob, when faced with three white guys approaching his doorway, was just trying to keep the Russians out. When I first moved to Dàlián, all the Chinese thought I was Russian. During one evening in a roast duck restaurant with two American friends, the waitress handed us a menu written in Chinese. When I told her we couldn't read it, she brought us a menu printed in Cyrillic. When I told her we couldn't read that either, she looked at me and exclaimed "what is your problem?!" Until my American coworkers and I arrived in Dàlián, most of the Caucasians seen in Dàlián were Russians. When several on-duty cabbies waved me off and refused to stop, I started to inquire about what the Chinese thought of the Russians. My unofficial and unrepresentative poll of three Chinese told me that they like the Russians less than they like the Japanese because they have no money, but it's also possible that the Chinese dislike for the Russians stems from the Russian occupation of Dàlián from 1898-1905, and then again during the Soviet occupation from the end of World War II until 1955. One Dàlián native with an American passport who ran a now-defunct cocktail lounge that I later found out was supposedly a front for drug smuggling, told me that the Russians who visited her place tried to negotiate down the published price of 20 RMB ($2.50 at the time) for a beer. From then on, I told the cabbies that I was an American, which was a new thing for me because American foreign policy in 2007 made it embarrassing to be an American everywhere else in the world.

No matter what the Chinese think of the Russians, the Russians continue to visit Dalian to study, work, and play. But sometimes the definitions of "work" and "play" can get a little blurry. Besides the Russian hotties such as my friend Kate – fluent in Russian, English, and Mandarin and employed by the U.S. Chamber of Commerce – who earn their money with their brains, there are others who earn their pay with their bodies. According to some Dàlián natives I met out on the town one evening, the Russian women are "very good dancers" and "very pretty" and "pretty young", so by putting 1+1+1+1 together, I'm assuming there was probably a pole involved, but it never included this one. Besides the Russian dancers, there were the Russian hookers who gave the rest of the white women in Dàlián a bad name. I know of one Irish woman, fluent in Chinese, who was in a Dàlián on a business trip and in an elevator when two Chinese guys stepped in. As the doors closed, one Chinese guy said to the other, "She must be one of those Russian hookers we're going to meet up with later on tonight…" The Irish woman replied in perfect Chinese, "I am not a Russian hooker." Horrified, those two guys couldn't get out of the elevator fast enough.

In case anyone was wondering, the Russian hookers fetched top dollar because they were considered by the Chinese to be the most exotic. The Chinese hookers in China, on the other hand, were almost a dime a dozen. Getting down to details, I was once told that a Chinese hooker goes for 600 RMB per night (girl keeps 400 RMB, rest goes elsewhere) but one data point does not indicate a trend, and that was a few years ago before inflation became a serious problem. But for those guys with a wad of cash to blow, in 2008 I was told that it was possible to get two very pretty live-in Chinese girls for two years for 3 million RMB ($450,000 at the time). Not an insignificant sum of money, one could only wonder what they would get in return. When I asked my Chinese friend, "What do they do for two years?" his reply was a very quick, "I don't know!" Since the Chinese can be circumspect when talking about such details, I bet he was trying to tell me, "I don't know what they don't do..." For the record, if a white guy needs to actively search for a Chinese hooker, then he must be in some pretty sad shape because white guys in China are natural hooker magnets. In fairness to the Chinese and contrary to many stereotypes, not all Chinese girls are hookers prowling for white guys, their cash, and a passport other than Chinese.

While on the subject of pretty girls, it was a nice surprise to learn that Dàlián and Northeastern China are famous for their tall, pretty girls. So much so, China's first modeling school is located in Dàlián. When my American coworkers and I, most of us single at the time we moved to Dàlián, discovered that little gem of information, we figured that our "hardship" assignment was going to be anything but. Call me crazy, but it only seemed natural for a 6-foot-plus, 190-pound white guy to be cruising the town with 6-foot tall, 110-pound Chinese girls wanting to strut their stuff. Because there are so many pretty girls in Dàlián there is a perpetual model glut, which is not necessarily a bad thing. I met one Chinese girl who modeled wedding dresses in her free time for 100 RMB (just over $12 at the time) per day. With pay like that, it's a good thing models don't eat very much.

But one girl's glut is one man's opportunity. As the story goes, a former Dàlián government official realized that Dàlián had a large number of pretty girls relocating to the city to attend the modeling school, but after graduation most had nowhere to go and nothing to do since not all of them could possibly be employed as fashion models. Since an idle body could become the devil's workshop, the government official, bless his soul, hired the jobless models as traffic cops dressed in short sexy skirts. This all seemed perfectly mighty fine in theory, but the traffic accident rate in Dàlián, if even possible, increased dramatically once the girls took to the streets. The girls are still out there, but now in more conservative dress. Today, Dàlián is also famous for its mounted policewomen, a contingent of hotties on horses. During the first "Summer Davos", hundreds of traffic cuties were out in full force, a couple of them every 150 feet for the three miles on Zhōngshān Road (中山路) between the Dàlián Convention Center at Xīnghǎi Square (星海广场) and the hotel housing the attendees. It's the most attractive police force I've ever seen, and a vast change from the gun-toting lesbians in Portland, Oregon. One well-connected Dàlián native told me in 2007 that for every 1,000 women who applied to become a traffic officer, one was invited to join the force. It was nice to see that the city has high quality standards.

In August 2008, it appeared that one traffic cutie was working a little overtime because the talk of the town was about how she, a civil servant, drove to work one day in a Range Rover valued at approximately 1 million RMB ($146,000 at the time). Of course, everything could be legit, but if the scuttlebutt on the street was any sort of barometer, it seemed that this particular policewoman might have been mounting more than just horses. When I asked another well-connected Chinese friend about the policewoman, the Range Rover, and how a policewoman could afford such a vehicle on government pay, they quickly exclaimed, "They're not hookers!" When I indicated that I didn't say anything about hookers, my friend paused for a second, stared at me with sad, disappointed eyes, and said, "You tricked me..."

While on the subject of mounting, many of those bodies for the Body Worlds displays seen in museums around the world were exported from Dàlián. According to the August 6, 2006, *New York Times*, with "little government oversight, an abundance of cheap medical school labor and easy access to cadavers and organs" Dr. Gunther von Hagens, the brains behind the Body Worlds exhibitions, opened up a large-scale assembly-line operation in Dàlián in 1999 to prepare bodies for the show.[8] So, when traveling to Dàlián, it's probably best for everyone keep their noses clean, lest someone ends up in a museum.

But before trying my hand at suspended animation, I was hoping to hit it big on the Chinese soap opera scene. I hadn't resided in Dalian for 24 hours and I was on my way to soap opera stardom. There we were, me and my boss' wife – the token white couple in the background of the scene – in the city's one decent western restaurant at the time, sipping Coca Cola and pretending it was red wine. At the table between us and the cameras was a very pretty girl with an older, squared-jaw Chinese man who was playing the role of some sort of police tough-guy. We didn't know the story line, and for all we knew, they were complaining to each other about how the white people were ruining their city by jacking up the cost of living.

After my soap opera gig fizzled out as quickly as it started, I was left with trying to cash in big with a career in Chinese movies after hearing by word of mouth about the need for foreigners for a movie production. In June 2008, a Taiwanese film crew came to Dàlián to film "Love at Sun Moon Lake" (爱在 日月潭), a television series with actress Lín Xīn Rú (林心如) aka Ruby Lin, Taiwan's answer to Mary Anne from "Gilligan's Island". This production was a work of fiction on many levels. Our scene was set on Dàlián's Russian Tourist Street at 5 a.m. and I and a dozen foreigners – Brits, Russians, Aussies, and Americans – were supposed to play out an open air market scene in Paris. My "wife", played by a British woman I didn't know, and I were supposed to be a French couple walking through the market with our "daughter", an impossibly-cute half-Chinese,

---

8   Barboza, David, "China Turns Out Mummified Bodies for Displays", the *New York Times,* August 8, 2006. http://www.nytimes.com/2006/08/08/business/worldbusiness/08bodies.html?sq= dalian body&st=cse&adxnnl=1&scp=1&adx nnlx=1313266310-KiBm0S5h7TVOKrwiySvn4Q

half-American 7-year-old girl holding a bundle of red balloons, while Ruby walked by with a stick of French bread poking out the top of a grocery bag, the bread being the most French thing on the entire set. If you go to the beginning of Episode #27, where the scene follows stock footage of the Arch de Triumph and the Eiffel Tower, you can judge for yourself if we each earned our $15.00. At the end of our performance, our Chinese contact who went by the name Lucy Liú, said the director wanted to know how many kids I had since role playing a father seemed very natural. Father? I was barely able take care of myself: during my three and a half years in China, I cooked only one meal.

And during those three and a half years, I never had to resort to an emergency visit to the Singaporean-owned Doerte Foods facility in Dàlián to pick up some meals-ready-to-eat (MREs). Many people have never heard of Doerte Foods,[9] but a Chinese friend of mine who once worked there as an administrative assistant told me that the Dàlián facility supplied MREs for American troops in Iraq and Afghanistan. Now, given all the anti-China sentiment and paranoia within the U.S. over a rising China, poisoned food, leaded paint, and deadly toys, it would definitely be an inconvenient truth if the U.S. government was relying on the Chinese to feed U.S. soldiers.

But each MRE exported out of Dàlián is yet another contribution to the city's and China's gross domestic product (GDP). Even though Dàlián's gross domestic product increased by an eye-watering 153 percent from 2001 to 2007, with 22 percent of this increase occurring between 2007 and 2008,[10] it looks like Dàlián's leaders have a good thing going that has many years left before it plays itself out. By the time I left Dàlián in May 2010, the population increased by almost 20 percent to about 6.13 million people,[11] and Westerners were not as rare as they once were

9   http://www.militaryfoods.com
10   http://www.starmass.com/china_review/city_overview/dalian.htm
11   http://english.dl.gov.cn/info/156788_192092.htm

now that multinational companies such as Goodyear, Intel, and Volkswagen, and their supplier bases have spent billions of dollars setting up or expanding their factories in Dàlián. With over 1,500 Western expats, the Dàlián American International School that didn't have enough kids to fill all grades in 2007 is now bursting at the seams. In 2009, according to the *China Daily*,[12] Dàlián's GDP reached 441 billion RMB, an increase of 15 percent over 2008 and one percent higher than government forecasts; and the city recorded an increase in industrial added value of 173.3 billion RMB, or a 17.5 percent increase over 2008.

As the GDP continues to grow, Dàlián's people were getting wealthier: in 2009 the average annual per capita income for the urban residents increased by nine percent over 2008 to 19,090 RMB, while that for the rural residents was 11,190 RMB, an increase of 14 percent over 2008. Since I repatriated almost three years ago, Dàlián's airport has doubled in size to almost 30 gates; a subway system is under construction; high-rise apartment buildings continue to sprout twenty at a time like mushrooms; new Chinese university campuses seem to appear overnight; a new deep-water port is under construction for all those DSIC freighters to return to; and a monster train station that will be the terminus of the high speed rail that will halve the travel time between Dàlián and Shényáng (沈阳) to two hours is about half-finished. Some people may see this as an economic bubble, but after living and working in Dàlián, I'm confident there's no bubble. There's still plenty of growth to be had if Dàlián is striving to become a Tier 1 city.

Through 2011 and 2012 when I returned to Dàlián for several visits, I would long for the good ol' days back in 2007 when life in Dàlián seemed simpler yet more complicated. Simpler because all I had to navigate were the Chinese and not all the new foreigners; but more complicated because I had to navigate the Chinese. If I wanted to do an expat assignment in a Chinese city

---

12   http://dalian.chinadaily.com.cn/2010-05/11/content_9818537.htm

that resembled an American one, then I would have never gone to China. Having spent a fair amount of time in Tier 1 Chinese cities, I'm not so sure that a multi-year assignment in one would have been as fulfilling or as mentally stimulating as venturing into the Tier 2 and sometimes Tier 3 cities. Dàlián and its people did not fail me when it came to providing interesting challenges, amazing adventures, and more "what the fuck?!" moments than I can count. Hookers, movie stars, leggy fashion models, drug smugglers, Japanese geezers on the prowl, sexy cops, body parts factories, and good friends – all wrapped up in one smokin' hot economy. That sure as hell wasn't the Manchuria I learned about when I was in the eighth grade.

CHAPTER 3

CHOOSING MY CHINESE NAME

WHEN IN KINDERGARTEN AND LEARNING HOW TO SPELL MY NAME, MY teachers and friends told me that my name – Rydzewski – was way too long. Since there are only nine letters, I never really understood their problem. During my high school years, some of my class-mates were named Anagnostopoulos (15 letters), Sandvoss (8), Papineau (8), Sokalski (8), Hollinger (9), Prashaw (7), Derouchia (9), Catanzarite (11), etc., and my teachers never had any problem pronouncing or spelling their names. Looking back, I think my teachers and classmates were simply afraid of consonants.

Years ago I resigned myself to the fact that because my name was supposedly too long, everyone will mispronounce or misspell my name, but I was pleasantly surprised that I never had to spell my name while living in Israel. I would simply say 'Ryd-jes-ki' and because Hebrew has a phonetic alphabet, the locals would just string together a couple letters. The cool part was that most Israelis strung together the same three Hebrew letters. The Israelis also made me feel at home because they were able to pronounce my name, which probably has plenty to do with the influx of tens of thousands of Polish immigrants. In the U.S., not so much: I had one manager who mispronounced my name for the six years I reported to him. I didn't bother to correct him because I just didn't care that he didn't care. He was eventually downsized.

It might seem odd to some that I'm reflecting back on my name now that I've had it my entire life, but this was an extension of my thought processes when I wandered the halls in one of my company's Chinese offices, visited five-star Western-style hotels, or businesses that catered to foreigners. I always wondered why and how the Chinese people came to be known as Sally, Lillian, Eric, Maggie, Sophia, Annie, Emily, Jennifer, Flora, Amanda, Jason, Jeffrey, Stella, Jessie, Andy, James, George, Emma, Richard, and other nice, safe, run of the mill Western names straight out of the Caldwell Township, Iowa, telephone book. What I found curious was that the one name that was always missing was "Amy" even though it seems that all American-born Asian women I've met are named "Amy". Amy is a cute name and when it's stuck to a cute Chinese or Asian girl, it only magnifies her cuteness. But during my three and a half years in China, I met only one Amy, which makes me think it's a phenomenon only among the American-born Asians. So I took it upon myself to set things right. While talking with a Chinese college co-ed on a train from Níngbō (宁波) to Shànghǎi in 2007, she pressed me to give her a "good Western name." Of course, I suggested "Amy". It stuck. With one down, I had only a couple hundred million more to go.

While many Chinese adopted what could be considered "typical" Western names, it was easy to spot those who were watching too much American TV given the number of people named Rachel, Chandler, Phoebe, Monica, Will and Grace. Then there are those who took on names that sometimes required a head-scratching double-take and one's best poker face. In one Shànghǎi Starbucks Coffee shop I was served by a girl named "Shaky"; I was once copied on an email addressed to a Chinese guy in Sìchuān Province who called himself "Dracula"; and Xenia, the cutest warrior princess I ever met, assisted me with my Chinese immigration when I first moved to China. I also met a guy named

"Texas" who probably figured no one would mess with him; and a girl named "Puppet" which makes one wonder if she was referring to the string, finger, or hand kind. At other various Starbucks shops around China, I saw a girl named "Windy", a girl named "Rainbow", a guy named "Kaka", a girl named "Air", a girl and a guy named "Rain" and two different girls named "Kinky", which makes me think long and hard about how Howard Schultz, the Chairman and Chief Executive Officer of Starbucks, is planning on increasing revenues in China. Speaking about long and hard, I met an Irish woman in Shànghǎi whose husband worked with a Chinese girl who adopted "Vagina" as an English name. Then there's the Chinese kid who called himself "Pentium", which made me wonder if that poor kid should go into hiding for fear of being sued for trademark infringement by Intel Corporation, the maker of the computer chip by the same name. But all these names are probably better than that given by a Chinese businessman in Dàlián to his accountant, who he always referred to as "Fat Girl". This required everyone else to refer to her as "Fat Girl" when they were talking about her since no one ever knew her real name. And of course, how can I not give special mention to the clean-shaven, U.S.-educated-engineer-cum-Shànghǎi-businessman who goes by the name "Harry Qín (秦)".[13] Granted, William Shakespeare once wrote, "...What's in a name? That which we call a rose by any other name would smell as sweet..." but it would be somewhat uncomfortable making evening plans with Dracula; telling my friends that I was out on a date with Kinky; or bringing Vagina home to meet my mother.

At first, I found it odd to find that many Chinese take on Western names, but the Chinese consider it embarrassing if they cannot pronounce someone's name. To show courtesy to Westerners who may not know how to pronounce a Chinese name, the Chinese tend to take on Western names to keep from putting

---

13   "Qín" is pronounced "Chin".

foreign guests in a bad spot that could cause embarrassment or cause either party to lose face. I can understand this reasoning, but does this mean that the Chinese who have taken on Western names sold out to the West? Why should the Chinese subjugate themselves by taking on Western names to make things easier for the non-Chinese? There are 1.34 billion Chinese and just over 300 million Americans. Who should be catering to whom?

But as I kept watching and asking, I realized that there was more to the whole name game. When I was in Dàlián, I dated one of those tall, leggy, too-cute-for-her-own-good policewomen for which Dàlián is famous. By chance she happened to work in a vital statistics office where all births, deaths, and marriages are recorded and tracked, and government identification cards are issued. She told me that she once did a search of her own Chinese name and found 10,000 others (both men and women) who lived in Dàlián with the same two-character Chinese name. Of course, if I shared the same first and last name with 10,000 others in a 20-mile radius of my home, I too would do something to demonstrate my individuality and to say to the world, "Hey world! I'm over here!"

Even if they had a Western name, I preferred to call a Chinese person by their Chinese name rather than a Western name because I felt as though I was showing them more respect. Calling a Chinese friend or coworker by their Chinese name rather than their Western name demonstrated that our friendship was close enough that I would actually know their Chinese name. The same goes for me and my friends who know how to pronounce my last name. Quite some time after my policewoman friend and I went our separate ways, I saw her one day on duty and in full uniform with her coworker. When I called out to her by her Chinese name, her coworker seemed taken aback and my friend hinted that I should disappear quickly lest she need to explain to her coworker why some random white guy knew her Chinese name. But in the end, I found that calling Chinese people by their Chinese name was a valiant but futile effort because the Chinese referred to each other by their Western names.

What also made it hard for me to accept a Western name adopted by a Chinese person is that Chinese names, like those given to children by Western parents, have meanings behind them. Because every Chinese character has a meaning, sound, and tone, the name of a child automatically has a special meaning and sound. As for the most common first names, I found plenty of lists out there but none with names that I commonly encountered around China or which ranked the names by most to least common. When I asked Maggie, my Dàlián Chinese teacher, to search the Chinese language websites, she couldn't find a list that ranked names in order of popularity, so she spent a couple weeks creating a list of names from her peer group (born around 1982-1985) that reflected a more reasonable level of commonness compared to what I encountered while living and working in China. The ten common boy's names she found in August 2011, in no particular order, were: Míng (明, meaning: bright), Gāng (刚, firm, strong), Bīn (彬, having both appearance and substance), Yǔ (宇, universe), Jùn (俊, handsome), Fēng (峰, peak), Wěi (伟, big, great, mighty), Yáng, (阳, sun, male), Xuān (轩, high, lofty), and Dōng (东, east, master). The ten common girl's names she found were: Tíng, (婷, graceful), Lì, (丽, beautiful), Nà, (娜, fascinating elegant), Huì, (慧, intelligent), Lín, (琳, beautiful jade), Yǐng, (颖, clever and gifted), Líng, (玲, sound of jade), Fēi (菲, luxuriant), Ruǐ (蕊, "stamen or pistil"), and Jīng (晶, crystal, brilliant). From the sounds of it, Chinese parents are naming their hermaphroditic children, Ruǐ (蕊). Western guys on their first trip to a Chinese hostess bar who think they have the girl of their dreams on their lap should make sure her name isn't Ruǐ. As for the most common family names, about 90 percent of the population shares only 50 different family names, while 50 percent of the population shares only ten family names. In Kentucky, this would be a bad sign. The top ten surnames, in order of most to least common are: Lǐ (李), Wáng (王), Zhāng (张), Liú (刘), Chén (陈), Yáng (杨), Zhào (赵), Huáng (黄), Zhōu (周), and Wú (吴).

All foreign expats who live and work in China are required have a Chinese name for their residence and work permits. The Chinese, who sometimes find it just as difficult to pronounce Western names as Westerners do Chinese names, would be more than overjoyed to give Larry Randall a Chinese name. But more likely, the Chinese government can't be bothered with a multitude of foreign names spelled out using the Roman alphabet because their computer systems can handle no more than three Chinese characters. Not just any three characters, but those approved and included in the official government database. According to the *New York Times*,[14] a 2006 Chinese government report stated that the Chinese Public Security Bureau's computers could at the time recognize only 32,252 of the approximately 55,000 Chinese characters. So, if an individual has a Chinese name that isn't in the computer, then they and some 60 million others need to change their names as China moves away from handwritten ID cards and standardizes on digital ones. If that weren't enough to limit one's individuality, the Chinese government, since 2003, has been standardizing the characters, including those for naming people.

I knew for quite some time that I'd need to come up with a name, but I kept putting off the inevitable. I'm sure (ok, I hoped) that my parents spent all nine months thinking about the perfect name for their first child and I didn't want to spoil their hard work by substituting it with a crappy Chinese name. Then again, maybe they didn't do such a good job picking my English name since "John" is a pretty boring name; they gave me my father's name (no creativity); and it's the name that prostitutes use to refer to their customers, albeit with a lower case "j". So, what to do? Did I want to be one of the 650 million people with one of the ten most common family names? I didn't want to imply in any way

---

14   Sharon LaFraniere, "Name Not On Our List? Change It, China Says", the *New York Times*, April 20, 2009. http://www.nytimes.com/2009/04/21/world/asia/21china.html?sq=chinese name&st=cse&adxnnl=1&scp=2&adxnnlx=1313355930-Fu8UgQrBr0XSSDVemEJlrw

I was a hermaphrodite from the Chinese equivalent of Kentucky. Besides, as a white boy, I don't really look like a Wáng, Zhāng, Gōng, or Liú, and "Hung" isn't a Chinese word. I wanted to leave the right impression with the Chinese name I was going to be stuck with for life.

Stressing me out even more were all the other variables that should be considered when picking a Chinese name. Some names are based on ancient Chinese theories such as: the Yin-Yang, compatibility of the Five Elements (wood, fire, earth, metal and water), the number of strokes in each character, the Eight Characters that make up the Four Pillars of Destiny (two characters per pillar: year, month, day, and hour of birth) and the person's horoscope. Five elements? Strokes? Eight Characters? Pillars? Christ. I was fucked. Stage fright was setting in but all was not lost. In their very entertaining and insightful bestseller *Freakonomics*,[15] the authors told the story of two brothers: one named "Winner" and the other named "Loser" (known to his friends as "Lou"). Over time, Winner found himself in and out of prison while Lou had a successful career as a New York City police detective. Maybe Shakespeare was right about those roses after all.

Then one evening while I was still in Portland, I checked my email to find that Zoe, a colleague of the warrior princess cutie in Shànghǎi, was looking for my Chinese name. "Crap," I said to myself, as I took a sip from yet another glass of red wine. "This is where the rubber hits the road. It's time to get creative." I surfed around some of the Chinese language resources and cobbled together some characters. Once I was happy with my selection I hit the ENTER key and those three characters jetted at the speed of light into Zoe's inbox. I asked her to reality-check my name to make sure I didn't choose the Chinese equivalent of Texas, Puppet, Shaky, or Kaka. A few minutes later, Zoe's reply landed in my inbox:

---

15 *Freakonomics: A Rogue Economist Explores the Hidden Side of Everything*, Stephen D. Levitt and Stephen J. Dubner, Harper Perennial, New York, New York. 2009

"I think your Chinese name is good. It has a good meaning in Chinese. 伟 is your last name. It stands for the great. 突 means outstanding.[16] 龙 is the symbol of luckiness in Chinese." For those who can't read Chinese, 伟 is pronounced *Wěi*, 突 is *Tū*, and 龙 is *Lóng*. My Chinese name — as immortalized within the infinite bureaucracy of the People's Republic of China — is *Wěi Tū Lóng* (伟突龙). If only my teachers and classmates could see me now. Their prediction came true: my name is *Wěi Tū Lóng*. Shakespeare, Levitt and Dubner may be right about names, fates, and roses smelling just as sweet, but it's going to be hard for anyone to forget a 6-foot-4 white guy in China named *Wěi Tū Lóng*.

---

16 I later learned that *Tū*, 突, really means "sudden", which makes me think that Zoe was just being polite, and I ended up with a nonsense name after all.

CHAPTER 4

HIRING ASIAN FLIGHT ATTENDANTS SLOWS GLOBAL WARMING

BETH, THE NORTHWEST FLIGHT ATTENDANT ON MY DECEMBER 2006 Portland-to-Tokyo flight, lived for her job. I knew she was special by the way she shoved that chicken in front of my face. Someone once said that a woman's eyes are a window to her soul. For a brief moment, I looked deep into Beth's blue eyes and peeked at her soul. Nailed to it was a sign that said, "Don't fuck with Beth." It was going to be a long trip.

But a funny thing happened when I transferred to my Tokyo-to-Shànghǎi flight. All of a sudden, the flight attendants were friendly, talkative, and attentive. If I didn't know better, I thought I boarded the wrong plane. I looked around and saw the Northwest uniforms and the Northwest colors, but instead of Beth, the flight attendants on this flight were Chinese. If American manufacturing companies can outsource their labor to Asia, airlines should consider in-sourcing all their flight attendants from Asia.

I've spent more than my fair share of time flying. Airlines that come to mind are: Northwest, Singapore Airlines, Alaskan Airlines, SAS, Malaysian Air, United, Delta, Continental, China Eastern, China Southern, Air China, Sichuan Airlines, Piedmont, Lufthansa, American, Thai Airlines, Air Europa, Cathay Pacific, Air Canada, Air France, KLM, Eastern, Swiss, Air Philippines,

CHINA DIARIES & OTHER TALES FROM THE ROAD

Varig, Japan Airlines, Cebu Air Pacific, Asiana, Air Bagan, Korean Airlines, Aer Lingus, Southwest, China Airlines, Ryan Air, Shandong Airlines, Agean Air, Air New Zealand, US Airways, British Midlands, Olympic Airlines, Turkish Airlines, British Airways, Shanghai Airlines, Lao Airlines, and Malaysian Airlines. I went out of my way to avoid Chinese discount airlines OKAir, Deer Air, and Lucky Airlines. After all this flying, it was clear that the best flight attendants in the world were Asian.

The global, gold standard for flight attendants, hands down, is Singapore Airlines. All flight attendants should strive to emulate the Singaporean flight attendants. In a perfect world, all flight attendants would be Singaporean. If Singapore needed another export industry, it should be flight attendants. Next down the list are the Chinese and Malaysian flight attendants. I can also add Thai Airways and of course, I'd be remiss if I didn't mention the leggy ladies at Korean Airlines. Lufthansa is a contender even though a German female executive of an industrial components company in Dortmund once told me, "Germany isn't really known for its service economy." A true statement, but blonde hair and blue eyes can help make up for deficiencies in other areas. Next come the flight attendants at a couple of U.S. airlines: the Alaskan Airlines flight attendants always seem chipper and happy to chat; the Southwest flight attendants are friendly and always ready with a joke; and all the Continental Airlines employees, prior to their merger with United Airlines, worked hard, flew right, and were downright helpful and courteous each time I boarded their planes. I don't think it's a coincidence that Continental Airlines was one of those rare profitable airlines, which begs the question: Do friendly employees make airlines profitable or do bankrupt airlines make flight attendants angry and bitter?

At the bottom of the list, however, are the long-haul flight attendants such as Beth. But to be fair, I should not paint with such a broad brush. There are some exceptional U.S.-based flight attendants, but they're diamonds in the rough. For example,

Jackie, the Hawaii-based Northwest flight attendant I met on my July 2005 Portland-to-Tokyo flight, is still one of my favorites for being happy and personable; and not all of Beth's coworkers that day were cranky. Just the U.S.-based ones. There was one Japanese woman working the flight that same day who was a real breath of fresh air. It was too bad they hid her away in Business Class. Why are the first class flight attendants always assigned to first and business class, while the everyday folks in coach get stuck with the leftovers and the spoilers.

What's a spoiler? Anyone who has flown in the U.S. knows what I mean. She's the bitter witch who, after 25 years of pushing chicken and beef, still hasn't realized she hates her job although everyone around her has. She's the turd in the punch bowl. On a flight from Shànghǎi to Atlanta in July 2008, we hadn't even left the ground when Kathy, an Atlanta-based flight attendant became the spoiler while handing out dinner menus. "Read the menu so I don't have to say 'chicken or beef' a hundred times..." Then there was Diane, on my June 29, 2008, Portland-to-Tokyo flight, who chased me out of an empty corner near the rear galley where I was stretching my legs and studying my Mandarin lessons after a few hours into the flight. None of her coworkers had a problem with me and even engaged in small talk about our flight, etc. But Diane decided to open up with all barrels. As I walked back to my seat to avoid her wrath, she followed behind me and kept at it by asking me where I thought I was going. Understanding that she was flawed to the core, I just kept quiet and walked to my seat.

After hundreds of domestic segments in China, I had only one Chinese spoiler on a China Eastern flight from Dàlián to Shànghǎi. I was sitting next to an overweight French businessman who had the middle seat and whose tray table was jutting into his stomach. When the flight attendants were serving drinks, one motioned to the French guy and said to her coworker in Mandarin, "that man's stomach is very big!" Everyone around us was able to hear the girl, so I replied in even louder Mandarin, "What? My stomach is very big?!" The girl, clearly shocked and embarrassed, said to me, "Oh no. Sorry" and went about her business. The French guy didn't understand Mandarin, and for all he knew I was asking the girl for ice for my orange juice.

For those who are not aware of the business model, most flight attendants need to fly around 80-100 hours per month (20-25 hours/week) to be considered a full-time employee. Those 80 hours can take the form of many short flights over many days, or a few long flights over a few days per month. Of course, to maximize the number of days off and remain a full-time employee, the long haul flights are very attractive and in high demand. The catch is that the flight attendants who choose those flights aren't. They choose their flight schedule and routes based on seniority, in the professional and literal sense. As a result, the overseas passengers normally get stuck with the 35-year veteran. Each time I encounter a cranky flight attendant, I still cannot figure out why someone who is so angry about their job and their employer insists on staying in their job. Life's too short to work a shitty job.

While discussing this topic with one Caucasian United Airlines flight attendant I met in Shànghǎi, she told me that all white American men have an Asian fetish. Call me crazy, but I think white American men, like most men and women from all walks of life, just want to be treated with some common courtesy and respect. The same goes for the flight attendants. As they say, what goes around comes around. When I was flying on what is now Delta's Portland-to-Tokyo route on September 30, 2010, I spotted from my exit row seat a businessman in his late fifties or early sixties a few rows in front of me with a much younger, cute, blonde-haired woman who turned out to be his daughter. We had not been on the plane two minutes before the man yelled at the flight attendant who, before we boarded, placed an object in the overhead bin that happened to be located above his seat. A couple minutes later, this same man began whining to his daughter, "why does he have more room" as he pointed at me. In an instant, the guy went from being a 60-year-old businessman to a 22-year-old asshole. For whatever reason, the purser upgraded this guy to a business class seat. During the flight, he returned to the coach cabin to visit with his daughter he abandoned, apparently to gloat that it's possible to get upgraded by being an asshole.

On the extreme end of things, some flight attendants also have to deal with the likes of Gerard B. Finneran, the then 58-year-old drunken investment banking executive who, while flying first class on a 1995 Buenos Aires-to-New York United flight, defecated on the drinks cart after the flight attendants cut him off; or the mad shitter who, on the same San Francisco-to-Shànghǎi flight as the United Airlines flight attendant I met in Shànghǎi, opted to defecate on the floor of the restroom instead of in the toilet. Savages. All of them. Maybe airlines should increase airfares just to price out the riff-raff. Just remember to wear your shoes when you need to use the toilet on any flight, since you never know what may be lurking behind the door...

In September 2006, I met a Chinese man who owns his own business. He travels into the Chinese countryside to find people who hold the Chinese equivalent of a high school education, and then contracts them out to companies in Japan to do jobs that the Japanese won't do. This is not much different than the Israelis who hire the Palestinians to harvest their crops; or the Malaysians who hire the Burmese and Bangladeshis to work in dirty manufacturing; or the U.S. who hire the Mexicans and other Latin Americans for all sorts of hard labor. It just went to show that everyone has a pissboy. In the case of my Chinese friend, the Japanese hire the Chinese villagers for three-year contracts. At the end of those three years, each Chinese laborer will make the equivalent of thirty years of Chinese wages. When they return to their village, they bump up into the middle class, buy an apartment, get married, have a kid, and try to live happily ever after. My friend should diversify into flight attendants. I was once told by another Chinese friend that many of the hookers in Dàlián hail from rural

Jílín (吉林) Province, about a day's drive north of Dàlián and also famous for its beautiful women. As the story goes, they move to Dàlián when they are around 20 years old, work for eight years, then return home with a load of cash to buy an apartment and to start a new life. Before I could finish the mental math – eight years; 400-1000 RMB per trick, give or take; living expenses; 1 million RMB to buy a home, etc. – my Chinese friend quickly summarized with "not clean."[17] Serving chicken at 38,000 feet in a toothpaste tube sounds much more appealing.

If airlines are looking to save money, they should replace all the over-priced, over-age, over-weight and over-cranky U.S.-based flight attendants with young, friendly, and attentive Asians. There is no reason why a U.S.-based flight attendant should ever be working on flights that originate or land in an Asian country. Seattle-to-Tokyo, Portland-to-Tokyo, Chicago-to-Tokyo, routes should have only Japanese flight attendants based in Tokyo; the Seattle-to-Běijīng and Chicago-to-Shànghǎi routes should have only Chinese flight attendants from China; and the San Francisco-to-Seoul route should have only Korean flight attendants from Korea. Western flight attendants should never fly on any intra-Asian (Tokyo-to-Manila, Tokyo-to-Shànghǎi, Běijīng-to-Tokyo, etc.) operated by a Western airline. This should be a no-brainer for airline management.

Insourcing flight attendants from Asia would be no different than the Chinese insourcing Western commercial airline pilots from other countries. The Chinese airline industry has estimated that they are short approximately 15,000-20,000 commercial airline pilots, and to make up the gap in qualified pilots they are insourcing Western pilots to resolve it. The U.S. carriers need to realize they have a problem with their flight attendants and should consider insourcing. Of course, there are plenty of recent American college graduates who can't find work that could serve as a

---

17   This was later confirmed by a Dàlián cabbie in July 2011 who thought he was doing a public service by warning me away from hookers over 20 years old.

labor pool for the airlines, but they would rather travel on a plane than work on a plane. Insourcing flight attendants from Asia would be a big step toward a better quality of life for many reasons:

1. The skies will once again be friendlier and prettier. It would be nice to step onto a plane and be greeted by a pretty, smiling face rather than....well, you know. Happy customers become repeat customers.

2. Asian flight attendants will probably be paid less than their American counterparts, but more than their native peers. This would encourage plenty of Asian women to become flight attendants, ensuring a constant supply of new talent when some realize that it's not their cup of tea.

3. On one trans-Pacific flight from Seoul to San Francisco, I estimated the cumulative weight of the flight attendants to be about one gross ton, with emphasis on both "gross" and "ton". Hint: the lap belt at the flight attendant jump seat shouldn't ride at breast level. Asian flight attendants are, on average, smaller than the U.S.-based flight attendants. The lighter an airplane, the less fuel the plane consumes.

4. Lighter flight attendants will be beneficial to the environment because using less fuel also means less jet exhaust, a reduction in greenhouse gases, and slowing of global warming, which will slow the melting of the polar ice caps. Even the polar bears that survive by walking on the ice will be happy since they won't die prematurely from drowning.

5. Smaller flight attendants will also help fight global terrorism, since using less fuel means less money in the pockets of the oil-rich nations that tend to host the fundamentalist groups responsible for senseless killings around the world.

6. The hiring Asian flight attendants will improve their understanding of the Western world. Putting them to work as flight attendants for a few years would allow them to learn about the world by traveling around it and by talking with people from all walks of life. In turn, they will become more efficient and effective players in the global economy and build the skills necessary to work in one of the many multinational companies expanding into Asia. In the long run, hiring Asian flight attendants could increase profit margins of many American companies besides the airlines.

7. Creating a more international flight crew would be good for American passengers, especially those who normally fly the Omaha-to-Denver route. We now live in a global village and those who live outside the U.S. will have a greater impact on the future of the U.S. than those within the U.S. Has anyone noticed the number of Asians showing up in American television programs and commercials? Is it a coincidence that an African-American actor played a U.S. president on a popular television series before Obama took office? It's psychological priming at its best.

Sourcing flight attendants from Asia will make the world a better place. Hands down. Everyone wins: the passengers, the airlines, the Chinese college graduates, the airline stockholders, Greenpeace, and even the polar bears and other wild animals. That is, everyone except for the terrorists, and we should be ok with that. Even Beth — my ray of sunshine — will be a happy camper because she will no longer need to don a not-so-flattering polyester uniform to hand out mediocre chicken or beef dinners to a mass of humanity with champagne expectations flying on a beer budget.

CHAPTER 5

SAY WHAT?!

IN SEPTEMBER 1991, WHEN I WAS ONE OF THREE AMERICAN WHITE BOY engineering grad students in a laboratory of twelve – the others being Indian and Chinese – the writing on the wall said that changes were brewing over the horizon. But, at 22 years old and never having strayed too far from my hometown of Massena, New York, population 10,000, just a mere 20 miles from my university, I did not have the perspective and foresight to realize how significant those changes were going to be or how much they would eventually impact my life.

During those days in the lab, I not only listened to Mandarin, but occasionally picked up one of the Chinese language newspapers left lying around the office to look at the photos. The pages, for all intents and purposes, were filled with mumbo jumbo. Then one day – I wish I could attribute it to foresight – I decided that I wanted to learn Chinese. How cool would it be to be a white guy who could speak Chinese and read that Chinese newspaper? I'm not impressed very easily, but for some reason I'm very impressed by white people who are fluent Mandarin speakers. Maybe it's because of the novelty, or because those people seemed to have transcended a cultural divide, as if those Mandarin-speaking white people cracked a secret code. After explaining my idea to a couple of the Chinese guys in the lab, they introduced me to the very patient and pregnant wife of another Chinese grad student who once taught Chinese to English speakers in Colorado. Each week during our one-hour class at her kitchen table, we would go through the basic basics: tones, pronunciation, and the "hello", "good bye" basics that wouldn't even qualify me as a two-year-old. In the end, I didn't get very far because my teacher had to care for her newborn baby; and the lessons did not really stick because once I left her apartment, I stepped back into rural Upstate New York, where many of the locals today still struggle with proper English.

Fast forward to September 2003. My job took me to China to qualify equipment and material suppliers for an upcoming expansion into the Middle Kingdom. During my maiden voyage into China, my coworker John and I pretty much relied on our two Mandarin-speaking coworkers for just about everything. We were grateful for their help, but being led around by the nose for two weeks left us none the wiser about the language, the people, or the country. John and I realized how white we really were when we first landed in Wūhàn (武汉) and couldn't even figure out how to get to our hotel. When I met a three-year-old Chinese girl in the back room of her father's stationary shop who spoke English and taught me Chinese while her father made up some business cards, I realized that I was not only white, but pathetic. This time around, the writing on the wall was loud and clear, and a drive through Wūhàn that showed an entire city under construction made it obvious that China was well on its way to becoming an economic superpower. In many subsequent trips to China for vacations or business travel, I made a point to learn enough Chinese to get around on my own so I didn't have to have China spoon-fed to me by those who wanted me to see what they wanted me to see. When I moved to China for my expat assignment, I promised myself that I wouldn't be as pathetic as the Swede who

John and I met in Shànghǎi who by then had lived for eight years in Běijīng and admitted that he couldn't speak any Chinese.

Formal language lessons aside, I learned most of my survival Chinese in Shànghǎi's bars and massage parlors. The best way to get over inhibitions about speaking shitty Chinese is to sip scotch while chatting with the girls. They would generally know some English and could help correct our bad pronunciation, but once they realized I had some basic knowledge of Mandarin, they would suddenly forget all their English. Years after leaving Shànghǎi for Dàlián, I still returned to the same Shànghǎi dive bar for language practice and to sip Johnnie Walker from the bottle behind the bar that, to this day, has the names of me and my friends on it. As for the massage parlors, there was no better way to practice Chinese than with Chinese girls rubbing our feet for $8.00 per hour. Formal, one-on-one Mandarin lessons in Portland, Oregon run about $40 per hour, so at eight bucks and a massage thrown in, how could I go wrong? I mean, when the girls were sitting at my feet and facing me, the least I could do was to talk with them to while away the time and to take their mind off the giant white feet jammed in their faces.

Native Chinese speakers, as they learn the Chinese characters, learn how to pronounce the words with one of the five tones: (1) high and steady; (2) rising tone; (3) high-low-high tone; (4) sharp downward tone; and (5) the neutral tone. Non-native Chinese speakers will not be able to tell just from looking at "你" that it is pronounced as "knee" with the second, rising tone while "好" is pronounced "how" with the high-low-high third tone. That requires some catch-up with brute force memorization. Still, Westerners can rest easy because, there is *Pīnyīn* (拼音, "join together sounds"), which is essentially the Romanization of the Chinese language that, in 1954, was accepted as an official form of Chinese. In 1979, to lessen confusion of various spellings of the same word, *Pīnyīn* was standardized to allow non-native Mandarin speakers to recognize that "你" is spelled *ní* with the tone mark over the "i" to indicate pronunciation with second tone; while "好" is spelled *hǎo* with the tone mark over the "a" to indicate pronunciation with the third tone. *Pīnyīn* has 21 initials (such as the "h" in "hao") and 33 finals (the "ao" in "hao"). To make a word, it's just a matter of combining the initials and the finals into one of the 693 (21 multiplied by 33) possible combinations, adding in the correct tones and calling it good. Piece of cake.

Almost. With over 55,000 characters but only 693 possible combinations of initials and finals − not including the tones − to get the meaning of a character, the math alone shows that there will be plenty of confusion. Since the Romantic languages (French − in more ways than one, English, German, and Italian) are not tonal, the biggest challenge faced by Western students of Mandarin is learning the tones. It's not too hard to imagine the outcome of a family dinner where a Chinese girl takes her American boyfriend home to meet her parents for the first time and he wants to say *mā* (妈) using the first tone, which means "mother" but instead says *mǎ* (马) using the third tone, which means "horse". This begs the question of what the guy who invented the word "好" thought about his mother when he invented the word thousands of years ago. No Oedipal complex there. Then again, it could be that he was trying to pull one over on his mother-in-law and to have the last laugh for posterity. Not learning tones or proper pronunciation may or may not get some people into trouble, but there's no doubt that they'll cause some serious confusion. While out shopping, it's important to keep straight the tones for *mǎi* (买, pronounced "my") which means "buy", and *mài* (卖, also pronounced "my") which means "sell". *Nǚ* (女, pronounced like "new") means "female", and *niú* (牛, pronounced "neew") means "cow".

When learning is fun, then it's easier to learn. When one Israeli coworker first showed up in Dàlián, he told me that he was interested in learning Chinese. I then asked him, "Igal, do you know the Chinese word for 'pork'?" He shook his head and waited for the answer: "It's *zhū*!" where *zhū* (猪) sounds very similar to

"Jew". "You gotta be shitting me," he deadpanned in that distinctly Israeli way. Who would have guessed the Chinese people thousands of years ago were early fans of Mel Brooks? Another one fitting of a Mel Brooks movie – or one written by Chris Rock and Jackie Chan – is "this" and "that", translated as *zhè ge* (这个, pronounced "jeh ge") and *nèi ge* (那个, pronounced "neh ge"), respectively. Many Chinese, rather than saying "ummm...." to fill a pause while thinking of what to say next, will say *"nèige nèige nèige..."* which, could cause some uncomfortable and possibly tense situations in mixed foreign company not versed in the language. This wasn't necessarily a filler word many white Westerners adopted while learning the language.

In the massage parlor, I learned that the word for "head" is *tóu* (头, pronounced "toe"), and the word for "toe" is, *jiǎozhǐ* (脚趾, pronounced "jee-ow-jer"). The word for "dumplings" is *jiǎozi* (饺子, pronounced "jee-ow-dze"), so it's important to not get these two words confused because if someone accidentally orders a plate of toes in China, they may just very well get them. While on the subject of food, when Chinese people line up for a photo they don't say "cheese!" which is *nǎilào* (奶酪, pronounced "nye-lao"), before the photo is snapped. Instead, they sometimes say *qiézi* (茄子, pronounced "chee-aid-dze") which means "eggplant", but allows for the same facial expression as if they were saying "cheese!"

If you like your eggplant spicy, you can then use the word for spicy, which is *là* (辣). If you like your women spicy, then you can say *là là* (拉拉)[18] which is Chinese slang for lesbian. Spicy spicy? I'm sure. When it comes to gender bending, many native Mandarin speakers when speaking English, get "he" and "she" confused. This isn't because homosexuality is more common in China than in the rest of the world (some Chinese believe that

18 The characters for "spicy" and "lesbian" are different, although the tone and pronunciation are the same. "拉拉" means "pull and draw" and is supposed to symbolize two girls walking hand in hand.

none of the 1.34 billion Chinese are homosexual), but because the spoken word for "he" is *tā* (他), and the spoken word for "she" is *tā* (她). Same same...but different. The formal translations for "lesbian" and "gay" are *nǚ tóngzhì* (女同志), and *nán tóngzhì* (男同志), which literally translate respectively into "female comrade" and "male comrade", wordplay not left unnoticed by non-members of the Chinese Communist Party.

No matter how much effort foreigners put into their Chinese lessons, there's always room for improvement. While stressing the importance of working in a team environment with one of my younger Chinese coworkers after discovering that she and another (male) engineer were regularly hostile toward each other, I wanted to say to her, "We're all in the same boat..." (*Wǒmen yīqǐ zài yīyàngde chuán*; 我们一起在一样的船")), but instead I said, "*Wǒmen yīqǐ zài yīyàngde chuáng*; 我们一起在一样的床 confusing *chuáng* with *chuán* to which she immediately shouted in English, "No! We're not all in the same bed!" One morning on my way to work, I made my usual coffee stop at the Starbucks in Dàlián's *Kāi Fā Qū* (开发区), or economic development zone. On this particular day, a couple teachers from Dàlián's Maple Leaf (Canadian) School were getting their morning fix before facing the kids. The teacher standing in front of me was a Canadian-born ethnic Chinese woman who wanted an apple muffin. In slow English to the guy behind the counter she said, "aaapppplllle muuffffinnn." She then repeated it because the guy was clearly unresponsive, and not yet awake even though he was surrounded by coffee. "Ap-ple", the woman repeated. Then, after a pause, she said, in confident Mandarin, "*Pì gu* (屁股)." I turned to her, smiled, then said to her in English, "the word for apple is *píng guǒ* (苹果). I don't think the ass muffin you just ordered will taste very good."

I like to think that the Chinese compensated for the overall difficulty of the language by making some things a bit more logical so marginal effort can vastly expand one's vocabulary. If someone learns to count to ten, then they can count to 99, since it's all just combinations of the same ten words. Add one more word, *bǎi*, 百, which means "100", and one can count to 999. Add another word, *qiān*, 千, which means "1000", and someone can count to 9,999. Add another word, *xīng qī* (星期, pronounced "shing-chee") and then one can say the days of the week. Add another word, *yuè* (月), which means "month", to say the months of the year. The word for brain is *nǎo* (脑, pronounced "now"); and the word for electric is *diàn* (电, pronounced "dee-an") so the word for computer is *diàn nǎo* (电脑), which literally translates into "electric brain". The word for light is *dēng* (灯, pronounced "dung") so the word for electric light is *diàn dēng* (电灯). The word for bubble is *pào* (泡), so a light bulb is, *diàn dēng pào* (电灯泡), or electric light bubble; and a blister is *shuǐ pào* (水泡), or water bubble. Pistachio nuts are called *kāi xīn guǒ* (开心果), which directly translates into "open heart nuts" but are commonly known as "happy nuts" because the partially open shell of a baked nut looks like a smile; "vacuum" is *zhēn kōng* (真空), which directly translates as "really empty"; and one worthy of the potty-mouthed Maple Leaf School teacher is *fēng pì* (风屁), which directly translates into "butt wind", but is better known to us English speakers as a "fart".

The best way to learn Mandarin is through complete immersion where one's survival is determined on their ability to communicate in Mandarin. The car company that provided drivers to me and my friends by default assigned English speaking drivers to all foreigners, but I fired mine and asked for a driver who spoke Mandarin and no English. By putting myself into a situation where I was limited by my own ignorance, I was forced to learn the language. I also made a point to travel to Chinese cities where Western tourists would not normally consider, and where English speakers were far and few between. Hunger and a full bladder are great motivators to learn Chinese. This was all on top of the six hours of one-on-one classes each week, talking with coworkers in the office and the Chinese migrant workers on the construction site at which I worked.[19] Of course, the tried-and-true method was to find a cute little BHD. BHD? "Black-haired dictionary" for those not in the know. Then again, my American friends who married Chinese girls tell me that their Mandarin has not improved because they relied on their wives to do the translating when they're out and about.

When I first landed in China at the start of my foreign assignment, I found myself limited to one-word sentences. Over time, one became two, two became four, and then four eventually became ten minutes of chit-chat. Since I arrived back in the U.S., a week doesn't go by where I don't hear, speak, read, or write Chinese with friends, the wait staff of a Chinese restaurant, or random people on the street, which just goes to show that even in the U.S., investing in Mandarin language skills will only pay dividends in our global village. These days, whenever I plan a trip to Shànghǎi, I make a point to seek out James, one of my grad school classmates from years ago. If we happen to meet for dinner, I do the ordering...in Mandarin.

---

19 It's been said that if migrant workers, other manual laborers, or little kids can understand a foreigner's Chinese, then the foreigner is speaking properly because these people are less likely to extrapolate poorly-spoken Chinese into something they can understand. On many occasions, I had Chinese friends translate my poor Chinese into good Chinese.

CHAPTER 6

CHINESE CHECKERS WITH LITTLE CHÉN

DURING MY FIRST VISIT TO CHINA IN 2003, I MET UP WITH AN AMER-
ican friend who lived and worked in Shànghǎi. Because he knew
I knew nothing about Shànghǎi or the various types of entertainment that could be found, he took me to Jùlù Lù (巨鹿路), a dark,
tree-lined street in Shànghǎi's French Concession. There, at the
time, were about ten different bars, side-by-side. Inside each bar
there were a half dozen or so Chinese girls varying from cute to
hot, none any more than 25 years old, and all watching us walk in
the door. Even with the air conditioning cranked up to full blast, it
was easy to see how things could heat up in a real hurry. That was
my introduction to the hostess bar scene.

There are some rules in the hostess bars. First, all the men are
invisible to all the other men and the Cowboy Code is respected: What
happens on the trail stays on the trail. There are no judges or juries
in these places, and there are no cross-examinations. The hostess bar
will test, stretch, bend, and possibly break any moral limits a person
may have set for themselves. Whatever that guy is doing with that girl
in that dark corner over there is their own business. That guy doesn't
need to answer to anyone but himself, and the chance of his wife
finding out is pretty remote because she's thousands of miles away in
their tidy suburban home looking after the kids.

In all honesty, I don't have patience for the bar girls mainly because they can be annoying. To them, I'm just a wallet with legs; a walking blue passport; a ticket to ride. A white guy walking in the door is like the Sugar Daddy Express pulling into station. If I did wander in with others, I would talk with the girls, practice my Mandarin, and play dice games. On that first hostess bar visit in Shànghǎi, I spent the evening talking with Maggie from Wǔhàn. Maggie was a high school math teacher by day (12 noon to 4 p.m.) and a cute little bar girl by night (6 p.m. to 4 a.m.) who lived in a cramped apartment with six other girls. Teaching alone wasn't enough to pay the bills to live in Shànghǎi and to help support her family, but Shànghǎi at the time offered more opportunities than Wǔhàn.

One evening three years later in Singapore, four of us found our way into Chinatown after dinner. In no time at all, we saw the tell-tale signs: a dozen or so small, dark, taverns along Duxton Road, with dessert lingering around outside and trying their best to tempt us into their establishments. We entered one place that was empty with the exception of the twenty or so hot little Filipinas who were on us like white on rice. Before we knew it, each of us had a girl on each lap, one on each arm, and one who provided a neck massage, and all aggressively competing for our attention and our money. All, looking like they just turned 20… or 18 for that matter…were dressed in the same style: short, tight, small, and just as easy to take off as it was to put on. There, a beer cost $10, and a night of drinking could quickly run into hundreds of dollars. After a while, we ventured into another bar where the girls pestered us to buy them drinks. "Buy me a drink? Buy me a drink. Buy me a drink!…" When I reached into my pocket and pulled out only lint because I didn't hit an ATM, I went from being the white guy to the wrong guy, and they all went away.

Although I couldn't even afford to buy a drink for myself, a couple of the girls didn't make me look like a total loser and sat with me to tell me their story: They answered an advertisement in a newspaper in the Philippines advertising "waitress" jobs in Singapore. The company flew them to Singapore, took their passports, handed them a bill for the airfare, and then put them to work in the bars. For every drink they sold, the girl would get half and the bar would get half. From the girl's take, she had to pay for her food, housing, discretionary expenses, the traditional remittance to her family back in the Philippines, and her airfare to Singapore. It doesn't take a finance whiz to realize that selling a dozen or two watered-down drinks per night was not a winning proposition. The economics of the situation – and Singapore's high tolerance of prostitution – incentivized the girls to get a little more creative about how they raised the extra cash.

While I was living in Shànghǎi in 2007 prior to locating to Dàlián, my friends told me they found a new Shànghǎi dive bar with atypical bar girls. Of course, I was a bit skeptical. Then one night, I followed them into their recent find. It was a narrow place with dark wood paneling more fitting of a traditional Dublin pub than a Shànghǎi dive bar. It was the kind of bar where it was cheaper to buy whiskey by the bottle than to order a drink at a time. By the time my friends walked the 15 feet from the door to the bar, Johnnie Walker, half the man he used to be, was standing proud on the bar in front of them. Behind the bar were glass cabinets with over a hundred of Johnnie's clones; Mr. Daniels from Tennessee; Mr. McCallan from the homeland, and their Japanese peers, each with Japanese and Chinese names scrawled on them with a fat black magic marker. The wood walls were plastered with Polaroids of Japanese salarymen in various stages of drunkenness, and there wasn't a white face to be found in the bar or on the walls. After a few seconds, it was clear that this was not an ordinary bar, and these girls were not bar girls, but just girls who worked in a bar.

Since the guys had been there before, they were already talking with the girls. English was not the first language of this bar, so each visit was a chance for us to practice our Mandarin. I started talking with one cute girl, Xiǎo Chén (小陈), or "Little Chén" who was standing behind the bar. In 2007 when we first met, she was between seventeen and eighteen years old, the third of six daughters of a rice farmer in central China, several hours south by bus from Wǔhàn. She wasn't alone in Shànghǎi and lived with her two older sisters. While the other guys talked with the other girls, I spent the evening practicing Mandarin and learning Chinese Checkers the hard way by getting my ass kicked by the seemingly innocent Little Chén.

In later visits to the same bar, I would always challenge Little Chén to a round of checkers. I would always lose. At first I would lose by 10 or 20 moves, and then after a couple of visits, I narrowed the loss to 5-10 moves. I did win one game, but I think she let me win. There's a reason it's not called "White Boy Checkers". I didn't care if I won. At least I knew she was spending time with someone whose intentions were benign and constructive. While sitting there playing checkers and for days later, I would always wonder what the future held for Little Chén. Spending twelve hours a day in a Shànghǎi tavern catering to foreigners is the last thing a teenage farm girl should be doing. But a job is a job, and a job meant money…

And money was needed to survive in Shànghǎi. If Frank Sinatra was Chinese, he would have crooned about Shànghǎi and all its glamour, glitter, and the billions of dollars sloshing around the town. Shànghǎi is full of stylish, cosmopolitan people in pursuit of riches. Thousands have been very successful, and they are not afraid to show it. After only two months of living in Shànghǎi, I saw a Rolls Royce, a Maserati, a H2 Hummer, four Ferraris in five days, and countless numbers of Audi A6's and 500- and 700-series BMWs. No self-respecting Chinese businessman would be caught dead in the BMW 300-series usually seen on the roads in the U.S. Conspicuous consumption permeates everyday living and Coach, Prada, Louis Vuitton, IWC, Rolex, etc., all do brisk business. There was a time when a Shànghǎi guy would impress his date by taking her to the Starbucks in the exclusive Xīntiāndì (新天地), literally translated as "New Sky/Heaven Earth") neighborhood popular with foreign expats where the wealthy Chinese and the wannabes go to see as well as to be seen; and where the foreigners can go for a dinner that doesn't stare back at them from the plate. In Xīntiāndì in 2007 when the Shànghǎi stock exchange was on its greatest bull run ever, it wasn't uncommon to see young Chinese couples with their his-and-hers laptops checking their stock portfolios.

The reality of it all is much grimmer. Although average annual salaries in China increased by 14 percent in 2006, and some college-educated professionals in 2010 saw 30 percent raises, the average annual per capita disposable income for a city dweller in 2009 was 17,175 RMB (about $2,642 at the time), up from 11,759 RMB (about $1,527) in 2006. By comparison, the rural population in 2009 had an annual per-capita disposable income of 5,153 RMB ($792), up from 3,587 RMB ($465) in 2006.[20,21] If any Chinese person could make it in Shànghǎi, they could make it anywhere, and from everywhere they come to give it their best shot

---

20   *Shanghai Daily,* March 27, 2007.
21   *China Daily,* January 1, 2010, http://www.chinadaily.com.cn/bizchina/2010-01/22/content_9361049.htm

to scoop up even a few crumbs because there's a better chance of collecting few crumbs there than back home in the villages. But to play the part, people need to look the part. So, how is a poor farm girl with a high school education from central China supposed to survive in a place like this?

An American friend of mine once told me about one of his experiences in a Shànghǎi hostess bar. The girl wanted him to buy her drinks so she could meet her revenue target for the evening. Like in Singapore, she kept half the take of what she sold. My friend saw that she was getting totally shitfaced, and he refused to buy her any more drinks. Instead, he said, "You just sit here, don't order anymore drinks for yourself, and at the end of the night, I will give you the cash you would have earned if you kept on drinking." The dollar amount was not a significant sum for a Westerner, but it meant whether or not the girl would be able to pay her rent, buy new clothes, or send money to her family in the countryside so they too can eat. This same friend once told me, "There are 1.3 billion people in China; you can't help them all," but he legitimately felt bad for the girl.

In this environment, what will happen to Little Chén? Since she spent most of her waking hours working in a bar, will she eventually gravitate toward one of the dozens of hostess bars in Shànghǎi that pander to foreigners? What will become of her if someone visits her little dive bar and starts looking for more than lessons in Chinese and Checkers, and lures her away with promises of easy money? Will she eventually end up like the Filipinas in Singapore? In Shànghǎi, there are an infinite number of ways to easily find trouble. Shànghǎi has ruined or ended more than a few lives. Will Little Chén become one of them?

As the Chinese proverb goes, "Give a man a fish and you feed him for a day. Teach a man to fish, and you feed him for a lifetime." Little Chén has a moderate grasp of English, which means that with more education and some computer skills she could become proficient enough to find a job as a secretary that would pay a respectable wage in a respectable job. If all went well, she could break free of the bar scene. But without outside help, this would be an almost possible feat because the tuition costs would eat up most of her income. From a Western perspective, the monetary cost to achieve this is insignificant, but to Little Chén it's an impossible feat. I could have easily walked to an ATM to withdraw at least her monthly income to try to solve the problem, but would that be the right approach, and would it solve the problem? I knew a couple people who had local Chinese "on the payroll", but would Little Chén be insulted if I offered to pay for her schooling? Would she think I wanted something in return? Or worse, would the offer push her toward the hostess bars where more Westerners could be found, thus more potential for more offers of generosity? As one American businessman, a 20-plus-year veteran of Shànghǎi, once told me, "All problems in China are fixable...with cash." But I thought I could teach Little Chén how to fish. After talking with a friend of mine in Shanghai who managed one of the city's five-star hotels, he arranged for Little Chén to interview for a job as a bartender where she could interact and practice her English with the visitors. He offered her a respectable job with plenty of opportunity for 3,000 RMB (about $400 at the time) per month, which was the going rate at the time in his hotel, but she turned it down because she could make more money in other bars in the city. It just went to show that it's possible to lead a horse to water, but you can't make them drink. Two years after we first met, I lost track of Little Chén after she left the little dive bar to work in another bar elsewhere in Shànghǎi that catered to the Japanese. It's anyone's guess of what became of her. Even more unfortunate is that Little Chén's story plays out tens of thousands of times each day in China, and over a million times a day around the world.

CHAPTER 7

'TWAS A 100-DEGREE DAY AT SANTA'S WORKSHOP

I MIGHT HAVE BEEN ABOUT SEVEN YEARS OLD OR SO WHEN MY MOTHER and her friends took me, my sister and some other kids to Santa's Workshop in North Pole, New York. Well, at the time, on that hot summer day, we thought it was the honest-to-goodness Santa's Workshop with giant candy canes scattered about, live reindeer that we could pet and feed by hand, prancing Elves, a cylindrical icy monolith glistening under the hot summer sun with a sign reading "The North Pole" hung over it, and the obligatory Santa Claus who must have been the new guy on the job because who the hell would want to wear a complete Santa suit in July? In June 2007 I drove past Santa's Workshop – just outside Lake Placid, New York, home of the 1932 and 1980 and Winter Olympics – on my way to the top of Whiteface Mountain. Santa's Workshop was still closed for the winter, and from the road it seemed much cheesier than it did a few decades prior. Sad and tired, like a three-legged dog, the place looked as if it would soon be closed for the summer, spring, and autumn too. Clearly, this wasn't *the* Santa's Workshop at *the* North Pole but *a* Santa's Workshop. Of course, if it was the real deal, Santa would have been riding heard on his elves, cranking out the goods in preparation for the next Christmas rather than sweating it out with all the hopeful rug rats who were trying to butter up the big boy well in advance.

For those not in the know, all the Christmas goods are really being cranked out of Yìwū (义乌, pronounced "eeeee-wooo"). Yìwū? Never heard of it? You may have never heard of the place, but everyone owns more than a few things that came from there. Yìwū, population 1.7 million and located a four-hour train ride south of Shànghǎi in Zhèjiāng (浙江) Province, is reported[22] to be home to 80 percent of the world's Christmas presents and most of the world's Christmas decorations. Although the Nazareth City Hall in Israel takes the redneck approach to Christmas decorations by keeping them up all year to stress its ties to Christmas, smart money has it that those decorations came from Yìwū. The world's Christmas capital is Yìwū, and Santa's elves are the chain-smoking Chinese migrant workers or farmers who traded in their tools for jobs in logistics, shipping, or sales.

---

22   http://www.ywhopeful.com/yiwu.htm

Logically speaking, it makes no sense for Santa's Workshop to be at the geographic North Pole. What man in his right mind would want to live in the dark for six months each year with penguins and polar bears when he could live in a warmer climate with a seemingly infinite supply of petite Chinese girls at his beck and call? In China, portly, unshaven white guys with grey hair can easily score with the cuties since those are signs of wealth, not age. Early one Sunday morning in February 2007 when I walked out of a Shànghǎi Starbucks with an American friend (who apparently seemed wealthier than I), a cute Chinese girl ran out of the store and after us, only to ask Bob if he wanted a "massageee". Unfortunately, after he politely declined, we didn't check to see if her name was Kinky, or if she was just starting or finishing her day.

When I first learned about Yìwū and its crucial role in the global celebration of Christmas, I knew I had to see it with my own eyes. After discovering that Yìwū is also the origin of half the world's socks, my trip became even more urgent. It's not everyone's idea of a sightseeing weekend, but I had to check it out just like some people travel to Cawker City, Kansas (or Darwin, Minnesota, depending on who you talk with) to see the world's largest ball of twine. My trip to Yìwū would make Clark Griswold jealous. Every time I mentioned Yìwū to my Chinese friends, they would say, "it's the place to buy small things," or, "you want to do some shopping?" They all knew about Yìwū, but none of them had been there. It was a famous place in China, but virtually unknown to many foreign tourists. With its 100-degree temps and 90 percent humidity, July makes for miserable sightseeing in China, but nothing was going to hold me back from this trip.

If someone was ever looking for a definition for a "shitload" then they need not look further than the Fútián International Trade City (义乌国际福田市场), Yìwū's premier attraction. In January 2006, the Fútián International Trade City was given an "AAAA" rating from the China National Tourism Administration, putting it on par with the Great Wall, the Terra Cotta Warriors, and the Forbidden City. There is a shitload of everything at Fútián, starting with square footage. In 2007, the market was spread over 10 million square feet on three levels, which is the equivalent of 175 American football fields. That made the Fútián Market at the time about two-and-a-half times the size of the Mall of America in Bloomington, Minnesota.[23] Unlike the Mall of America where a significant portion of the square footage is wasted on frivolity such as an amusement park, a food court, bars, restaurants, and walking space, Fútián is nothing but stalls – over 40,000 different stalls – all of them jam-packed with stuff. More specifically, that's 28 categories of stuff comprising of about 200,000 varieties of daily goods.[24] In China, wasted space is a wasted opportunity to make money, and the Chinese don't waste anything when there's money involved.

I wasn't carrying my GPS on this trip, but I had no trouble pin-pointing ground zero of the real Santa's Workshop. In July 2007, it was in the air-conditioned comfort of the third floor in the north end of Phase 1 of the Fútián International Trade Market. There, I found row upon row of vendors selling Christmas lights, Santa uniforms, a dozen or more types of fake Christmas trees, hundreds of types of glass Christmas tree decorations, a six-foot tall life-like Santa that played a saxophone and danced to Christmas music for 500 RMB ($66 at the time), garland up the wazoo, miles of Christmas lights, hundreds of Nativity scenes, and dozens of types of cardboard decorations with Santa's face and "Merry Christmas" written underneath it in English, French, and Spanish, but not Chinese. Not only were they selling things, but they were only selling things in lots of 1,000 or more. If you plan a trip to Yiwū, just remember that you can't buy just one fake tree with blinking LED lights built into the pine needles that's guaranteed to tweak out the epileptic in your family, but you would need to pick up a forest's

---

23   http://treehouse.ofb.net/go/en/place/183605
24   http://www.yiwucompany.com/yiwucompany/. For a map of this monster, go to http://www.yachina.com/index.php?page=yiwu_market_digital_map.

worth. Need to replace that Santa hat you lost last year at the company party when you snuck away with the hottie from finance? Be ready to pick up a Santa hat for everyone in the company. Have a friend who could really use a three-dimensional Last Supper clock for 4.8 RMB ($0.64 at the time)? Go find a congregation of at least 999 others who could use one too. If you can't fill a standard shipping container with stuff, then you're not worthy of a vendor's attention. Because I looked the part of a tourist and was one of the rare tourists there for sightseeing, Fútián was the first Chinese market I entered where the sales people did not harass me. If I wanted to ask a question of them, I had to work hard to get their attention. All the others – Americans, Indians, sub-Saharan Africans, Russians, French and other Europeans, and numerous Middle Eastern men, all fluent in Mandarin – were there for business. Every day of the week in 2007, before the Great Recession, over 1,000 shipping containers left Yìwū through Níngbō Port, destined for the four corners of the world.

There was plenty more to Fútián than just the Christmas decorations. There were several thousand stalls selling "hair accessories", half a floor selling "jewelry", and probably 500 stalls selling fields of plastic flowers and bushels of fake fruit, the kind of stuff that somehow finds its way to every grandmother's dining room table. One could buy enough Muslim prayer rugs to outfit the entire Middle East; hair brushes; late night TV regulars such as the 6-minute Abs exercise kit and the SaunaBelt; a hundred flavors of rubber rafts; decorative glitter by the pound; and freshwater pearls by the ton. There were other Muslim ornaments with "Allah" written in Arabic, images of the Virgin Mary, Jesus Christ, and Chairman Mao, all on the same store shelf. If you're fresh out of Divali[25] and Chinese Lunar New Year decorations, you can pick up more in Yìwū. They can be found near the shop that sells scale models of American colonial sailing ships. If you lose your

---

25 The Indian festival of lights.

keychain, I know where you can find about a billion replacements. I looked long and hard for Suzanne Somers, but couldn't find the ThighMaster. Instead, I found a store that had a universe's worth of snow globes in all shapes, colors, sizes, and themes.

At the time, the center of the sock universe was the Knitting Market on Huángyuán Road (篁园路), a hot, unassuming, dimly-lit warehouse without an air conditioner in sight. It takes a lot of socks to cover the feet of half the sock-wearing world and this place was easily up to the task. There, in a few acres of floor space, close to 3,000 different stalls sold socks for all ages in all sorts of colors, patterns, styles, materials, and sizes. Wandering among the vendors were a dozen or so potential customers who were touching, feeling, stretching, and/or pulling the socks for a quick quality check. A few vendors were taking orders, but the rest, in various stages of undress, were sleeping, chatting, or playing cards to while away the unbearably hot day. Since my trip to Yìwū, the Fútián Market – if it was possible to get any bigger – was expanded to make room for the sock market.

With my key missions accomplished, it was time to do some other exploring. I found the main Huángyuán Market (篁园市场) jammed with about 15,000 vendors selling 80,000 different types of everything, as well as city block upon city block of bra, underwear, scarf, mitten, glove, and hat shops. The more I walked, the more I found. I wandered into the dilapidated warehouse that was the Bīnwáng Market (义乌宾王市场). In the market itself, lighting was at a premium and the walls could have used a couple fresh coats of paint. The ceiling fans were working overtime, but the thick, humid air just didn't want to budge. Still, it was open for business, with people selling bath towels and neck ties and a dizzying array of goods. Need 2,000 feet of lace twenty feet wide for the world's largest dining room table? Bīnwáng was the place to go.

What was more astonishing was that after a full day of hopping around from market to market, I barely scratched the surface of what this little city had to offer. If I ever happen back to Yìwū,

I will make sure I leave more time to visit: the Electrical Home Appliance Market, Correspondence Market (pens, paper, stationary, etc.), Computer Market, Commodity Market (aluminum products, clothing material, ceramic building materials, stone materials, etc.), Goods and Materials Markets (building boards, lumber, hardware, paint, logs, bamboo, windows and doors), Furniture Market (home and office), Agricultural Trade City (fruit, grain and oil, vegetables, flowers), Producer Goods Market (Decoration material, plastics, metal material, construction material), Real Estate Transaction Market (houses), Cosmetics Market (various cosmetics, makeup utensils), Clothing Market (clothing, pile, non-staple), Food Market (non-staple foods, groceries, dry fruit, candy, roasted seeds and nuts), Bed Clothes Market (pajamas, knitted underwear, shirts), Textile Market (textile and cloth), Spectacle Market (eyeglasses), Cultural Goods Market (cultural goods), the Raincoat and Umbrella Market, Clock and Watch Market, Photo Frame and Picture Frame Market, especially the Adult Underwear Market, and the Knitting Raw Materials Market.

By the end of the day I was so overwhelmed with dehydration, the humid weather, and everything I saw that it all was just a blur. That evening, after I finished my sightseeing and was relaxing in the air-conditioned comfort of a Chinese coffee shop, I realized I couldn't remember much of what I saw. It was not until the next day on the train back to Shànghǎi when I was able to write down just a few of the things sold in the markets: there were shops that sold toothbrushes (for export), the plastic brides and grooms that populate the tops of wedding cakes, aluminum foil, moth balls, swimming goggles; inflatable swimming pool toys in all shapes, sizes and colors; hot water bottles (who uses those things anymore?), wax and soap flowers, all the stuff one can find in American arts and crafts stores, clothes hangers, jade jewelry, packing tape, glue guns and refills, mahjong tiles, shoe polish, and wooden back massagers and back scratchers.

There were straw hats, baseball caps, and a United Nations worth of plastic flags. I saw pantyhose, toy guns, belts and suspenders, vases, cups, plates, saucers, chopsticks, necklaces, snorkeling masks, rings, flip flops, earrings, silverware, Halloween decorations, suitcases, sneakers, sandals, every one of those plush toys you can't seem to win at carnivals, nylon thread that sold for 6 RMB for about a kilometer which amounted to $0.15 per tenth of a mile, fishing poles, and rubber gloves. No destination would be complete without Elvis, even a ceramic Elvis, who was joined by a ceramic Michael Jordan, and a whole jazz band of famous ceramic musicians led by Louis Armstrong and Dizzy Gillespie. There were binoculars and telescopes; still more underwear; lava lamps, plastic and steel abrasive cleaning pads; pots and pans, soup, nuts, and woven baskets. There was something for everyone and for every occasion. Except for sex toys. The Sex Toy Capital of the World is Wēnzhōu (温州), China. Who in their right mind could refuse to buy sex toys or "spice lingerie" from the Wēnzhōu Hawaii Electronic Science and Technology Company? Maybe that'll be my next trip...

Visiting Yìwū was more than just an adventure, it was an epiphany. It made me aware of why the Chinese annual GDP growth was a red hot 12 percent before the Great Recession and around ten percent after the Great Recession; and why the U.S. trade deficit with China remains in the hundreds of millions of dollars. Mind you, that's hundreds of millions of dollars at one 64-cent three-dimensional Last Supper Clock, and one perfect plastic apple, at a time. My trip to Yìwū also made me realize that the negative publicity concerning Chinese products is unwarranted. Over the last few years, there's been much propagandizing against the Chinese with respect to the quantity and quality of their products. The inconvenient truth is that when the Chinese are said to have "dumped" their products into the U.S., the Chinese are just not sending ship after ship to American shores with hopes that someone might buy the stuff. The Chinese like cash up front and all the stuff that arrives in the U.S. has already been purchased by buyers like those I saw in Yìwū.

The problem is that not all those buyers of potentially dangerous goods are doing all or any of the right quality checks. Everyone should trust, but verify. Some are, some aren't. The Chinese cannot be held fully responsible for the small parts in their toys that end up in the throats of American children; the lead that ends up in the blood of the same children; or the melamine[26] that poisoned family pets. Maybe we never hear about the defective sex toys that short-circuit because people learned to like that kind of thing. Weeding out poor quality rests squarely with the American buyers who import thousands of shipping containers of hazardous toys every year, trusting they're getting what they're expecting. But the buyer should also understand the risks associated with their purchases. For example, it's still possible to buy metal-tipped lawn darts in China for about $15 per set – my American friends and I briefly considered holding a beer drinking and Jarts party in Dàlián's Xīnghǎi Square, the largest public green space in Asia – even though they've been banned for import into the U.S. since 1988. In short, caveat emptor. Let the buyer beware because quality and safety checks sometimes get lost or forgotten in the deal making process.

When I returned from my trip, my Chinese friends and coworkers seemed disappointed that I left Yìwū empty-handed. But from now on, when Christmas rolls around and I see the decorations going up, or see a random guy in a Santa suit; or when I reach down to pull on a pair of socks, I will always give a knowing smile, and remember my most amazing adventure on that hot July day in the Zhèjiāng city of Yìwū.

---

26 Melamine is an industrial plasticizer used to boost the nitrogen content of diluted materials to hide that dilution had occurred. In some circles in China, it is also known as "protein powder". It has no nutritional value but causes kidney stones and its ingestion can be fatal.

CHAPTER 8

50 LESBIANS + 50 TSA SCREENERS EQUALS WHAT?

LET ME TELL YOU ABOUT DAVID M., THE RATHER FLAMBOYANT TSA officer at the Hancock International Airport in Syracuse, New York, who would probably be more comfortable in a cheerleader uniform (the skirt type) than his TSA digs. He swung his arms and legs with vigor when he told everybody in the 100-foot line to make sure they had their shampoo (he acted out washing his hair), toothpaste (acted out brushing his teeth), skin lotions (acted out rubbing the lotion on his arms and body), etc. in a one-quart Ziploc bag. When someone in line showed him their bag, David replied, "Well, that's a one-*gallon* bag, not a one-*quart* bag. That may cause you some troubles up there," as he pointed to the dozen or so bored-but-trying-to-look-official folks standing around the single X-ray machine. The passenger countered with, "I have already flown with this bag." David replied, "well...you can always try to see what happens..." Of course, he offered, the shop next to the security checkpoint sold one-quart clear plastic Ziploc bags for twenty five cents each.

When I was about thirty feet from the X-ray machine I thought David's antics were about to end, but he noticed that the guy in front of me had an airline crew badge. David approached him and, in hushed tones as if he was planning a jailbreak, suggested to the crew member that he could move to the front of the line. I'm all about making sure crews get to planes on time, so I had no issue with the suggestion. What made this noteworthy was that David said a few more words, the guy shrugged, remained in place, said something I couldn't hear but to which David replied, "I don't make decisions," before he went back to primping. If David was not making decisions, then what was the point of being a security screener? Something tells me that the TSA might have hired David more for entertainment value than anything else.

According to the Transportation Security Administration,[27] "All candidates must meet minimum qualification requirements established by law including: U.S. citizen or U.S. national; high school diploma, GED or equivalent, or one year of security or aviation screening experience; English proficiency; Pass a background check." If anyone can pass these requirements then they could be rewarded with salaries ranging from $18,000 to $40,000 as a security officer; or if they really hit the jackpot, $172,000 per year as a senior level officer. For comparison, $172,000 is only $58,000 shy of the salary for the U.S. vice-president.[28] By comparison, the average starting salary for a public high school teacher with at least a four year college degree and all the required state certifications is $31,507.[29]

So, what is a TSA screener supposed to do to earn as much (or more, depending on the locality pay) as a college-educated entry-level high school teacher? According to the TSA,[30] they provide "frontline security and protection of travelers, airports and airplanes by identifying dangerous objects in baggage and on passengers. Their job is to prevent those objects from being transported onto aircraft by utilizing diverse, cutting edge electronic detection and imaging equipment, as well as using the lessons

27   http://www.tsa.gov/press/releases/2004/press_release_0387.shtm
28   http://www.glassdoor.com/salary/tsa-salaries-e41347.htm
29   http://teacherportal.com/teacher-salaries-by-state
30   http://www.tsa.gov/press/releases/2004/press_release_0387.shtm

learned from a concentrated training curriculum." Clearly David, and his counterpart I encountered the week prior in the Detroit Metro Airport who whiled away his day singing 1960s television theme songs, deserved a pay raise for going above and beyond the call of duty. Then again, maybe all TSA officers should get a pay raise. On a 2008 trip back to the U.S., I was warned by two TSA officers (one in Detroit, one in Norfolk, Virginia), that I should take my money out of my money clip before putting it through the X-ray for fear of it not being there on the other side. When I said to both of them, "I thought you guys were security. My money should be safe, right?" they just shrugged. Then I asked the TSA officer in Norfolk, "you do not trust your coworkers?", and all I received was silence since the guy didn't know how to, or want to respond. To this day I still get cautioned by TSA to remove the cash from my money clip before putting it through the machine. If these guys don't trust each other to keep a few dollars safe as it goes through the X-ray machine, how can we, the traveling public, trust them to keep us safe?

TSA could learn a few things from the Chinese when it comes to respecting personal property. In 2008, I asked a coworker to bring from Portland to Dàlián what, according to the vineyard, was one of the very last bottles of wine of its kind in existence. Along the way to Dàlián, Wayne had to make a stop in Shànghǎi for some meetings. Because of a traffic jam, Wayne was so late getting to his plane that he had to carry his checked luggage onto the plane to Dàlián. The Shànghǎi Pǔdōng Airport (上海浦东机场) security promptly confiscated the bottle of wine and gave him a receipt. Knowing that another friend of mine was flying from Shànghǎi to Dàlián a couple days later, I emailed my friend a copy of the receipt and Wayne's passport information. The Shànghǎi Pǔdōng airport security took the receipt and passport information from my friend, and lo and behold, returned with my intact and uncorked bottle of wine that I later shared with my friend as a reward for rescuing it.

The TSA boys and girls could also use a few lessons from the Israeli airline security people, but one frigid glance from the lovely ladies of the Israeli Defense Force (IDF) would have them pissing their pants and running home to Mommy and their computer games. Those Israeli hotties don't take shit from anyone. Israeli security, prior to flight check-in, consists of a one-on-one interrogation for 15 to 30 minutes or so per passenger to sort out the terrorists from the innocents. That's in addition to the background checks conducted by the airlines the day prior to departure. The U.S. airline industry has balked at this type of security for fear of flight delays, privacy concerns, etc., but their claims are bogus. Americans just need to learn how to adjust – and show up earlier to the airport – if they want to be safe and to catch their plane on time. Besides, more airports are offering free wireless internet, so airport time needn't be lost time.

Then again, maybe the TSA officials in charge of staffing the security stations at U.S. airports should rip a page right out of the playbook used by China's airport security force who clearly took some tips from the Dàlián city official who hired the model school leftovers as traffic cops. Instead of skirts, the Chinese airport security cuties are dressed in a black battle dress uniforms (BDUs) like those more commonly seen worn by a SWAT or a Special Ops team, combat boots, and a wide, webbed-nylon belt cinched tight to accentuate their femininity. Hot. Instead of frigid glances, the Chinese girls carry hand-held metal detectors to give each passenger a very thorough secondary pat-down. I once forgot something in the back pocket of my pants, but was quickly reminded when the girl gave my ass a firm and lasting grip. Ever since, I would scope out the cutest metal detector girl. On occasion, I would chat with her for a few seconds while she's up close and personal during the full-body pat-down, not knowing whether I should leave a tip, ask her out or for a cigarette when she was done. How could someone not be psychologically primed to have a good flight after a security check like that? I bet there would be less anger in U.S. airports today if every trip started off like they do in China. Of course, I should be careful for what I wish for because after a few trips through Chinese security I started to believe that some of those metal detector girls aspired to join the Chinese National Ping Pong Team.

Back in Syracuse where a dozen TSA officers manned a single X-ray machine, it seemed that the TSA believes in quantity rather than quality. One flight attendant friend of mine told me that she and her coworkers say that TSA is short for "Thousands Standing Around". It is important to remember, however, that any number – no matter how big, thousands, millions, billions, infinity – when multiplied by zero, still equals zero. If David and the other 49,999 TSA employees are the first line of defense to protect the flying public from another September 11, then the U.S. air traveler is in a worse position now than prior to the attacks. I'm convinced that the TSA is purposely hiring the under- and poorly-educated to be screeners because the TSA is looking for robots to follow the rules without having to interpret those rules by using common sense. A shoe-bomber in London? That means all shoes on those over 12 years old must be suspect and should be X-rayed. Gels, liquids, and pastes in another bomb plot in London? It's time to ban all gels, liquids and pastes from carry-on luggage. This may make sense to someone, but it's absurd to think air travel is safer because we can only carry four ounces of liquids into the cabin. There are dozens of chemicals that, in quantities of four ounces or less, when used in the right way, could easily bring down a Boeing 747. Who needs box cutters when it's possible to kill someone with a ballpoint pen by jamming it through their eye and deep into their brain.[31]

According to the TSA, screeners are hired to not look for terrorists, but only terrorist contraband such as toothpaste, shaving cream, toenail clippers, deodorant, breast milk, etc. The irony is that while TSA is telling the 75-year-old grandmother that she has

---

31   Bal, R., "How to Kill With a Ballpoint Pen: Credibility in Dutch Forensic Science", *Science Technology Human Values*, Winter 2005, Volume 30, Number 1, pages 52-75.

to toss her one-ounce bottle of hand sanitizer because it wasn't in a plastic bag (as was done at Syracuse the day I encountered David) there are plenty of items native to a commercial airplane that, with a little MacGyver creativity, could be used as weapons. Opening the emergency door at 35,000 feet comes to mind. As the gun lobby likes to say, "Guns don't kill people, people kill people." So, who's looking for the people? Let's pose a question to see where TSA logic takes us: What regulation should be put into place if a terrorist swallowed a condom full of plastic explosives prior to a flight, only to retrieve the explosives during the flight to take down a plane?[32] Would that mean everyone would be required to have a pre-flight enema or X-ray? Which TSA folks do you think would get the honor of doing that cavity search? Hmmm…maybe yet another reason to bring over those Israeli hotties or to outsource security to the Chinese? The fact is that if a terrorist wants to take down a plane, they will go to all costs to make it happen.

By the time I finished a typical round trip from China to my mother's house in my hometown of Massena, New York, my stuff had been X-rayed three times in China, twice in Japan, once in Syracuse, and once in Detroit. Only in the U.S. did and do they still care about the taking off of shoes and carrying toiletries in little plastic bags (which I don't bother to carry or to volunteer them to X-ray because no one seems to mind); and only in the U.S. did the security people detract from the traveling experience with their immaturity and amateurish ways. The Chinese and Japanese security people treat travelers with proper respect. While the TSA are out taking lessons from the rest of the world on how to do their job properly, they should also make a stop in Tokyo, where all the guards – male and female – were polite, pleasant, and professional. In Tokyo, there were four screening

---

32 I'm not giving any help to the terrorists since drug smugglers have been using this strategy for decades, which seems to be a waste of time and effort: in July 2011, I carried two one-pound bags of white powder (fructose) from Portland, through Tokyo, and into China in my carry-on bag without anyone raising an eyebrow for the entire trip.

stations, all in use, and four guards – not fourteen – per station, each with a job to keep the line moving. Everything ran smoothly. During one transfer through Tokyo, I watched a Japanese security guard kindly and patiently help an American passenger work the three-dimensional jigsaw puzzle that became her makeup and lotions after he inadvertently removed them from her one-quart plastic bag.

When I think of TSA, I'm reminded of a paper tiger. A paper tiger, *zhǐ lǎo hǔ* (紙老虎), is a Chinese saying for something that is seen as threatening but is really harmless. Besides being a paper tiger, the TSA is simply a drag on the U.S. economy. It is yet another fat bureaucracy that needs feeding, taking resources away from more value added initiatives such as education. Then again if everyone had a college degree, then there wouldn't be anyone to apply for TSA jobs. I'm not against airline security, but against my tax dollars being wasted on airline insecurity and people who are empowered beyond their competency. Maybe Osama Bin Laden, killed by Seal Team Six in May 2011, won the war on terror after all.

So, who read this entire chapter just to read about the lesbians? You know who you are. As it turns out, there's an old joke that comes to mind each time I'm spending quality time with the TSA folks. Once in a while, I may share it with my fellow travelers in line, or the non-TSA local contractors hired to check IDs against boarding passes, depending on if they're the type of person who would appreciate such a joke. Here it goes: What do you get when you put fifty lesbians and fifty TSA workers into the same room? One hundred people who don't do...um, something. Well, former Vice President Cheney and Richard Nixon come to mind. Some will figure it out, and others may not. But don't worry, the joke is not derogatory toward homosexuals...homosexuals are people too. Speaking of people, the next time any of you are flying through Syracuse please send David my regards. If he's still employed with SYR TSA, you won't be able to miss him since I'm sure he'll still be washing, scrubbing, and rubbing himself with his infinite supply of invisible toiletries...

CHAPTER 9

BUMMING AROUND BORACAY

UNLIKE THE U.S. WHERE VARIOUS HOLIDAYS ARE SCATTERED throughout the calendar year, China concentrates most national holidays into two "Golden Weeks": the Lunar New Year in the January-February timeframe; and the first week of October to commemorate the founding of the People's Republic of China by Mao Zedong on October 1, 1949. The Golden Weeks, originally three of them until 2009 when the week-long communist May Day celebration was scattered across the calendar and into various long weekends,[33] started in October 1999 as a pilot program by the government to stimulate domestic spending through tourism.[34] In a typical Golden Week, some 120 million or so go on vacation, jamming up the trains, planes, and buses to visit tourist sites or distant family. In October 2007, this meant only one thing: it was time to get out of China.

Having spent the two previous Golden Weeks of 2007 in China, I was itchin' for a peaceful, tropical destination, especially since the crisp Dàlián autumn had arrived, signaling that winter was just

---

33 May Day, Tomb Sweeping Day, the Dragon Boat Festival, and the Mid-Autumn Festival.

34 http://www.canada.com/montrealgazette/news/story.html?id=10b7555b-e0ca-4bc0-9ffb-da127223e11d

---

around the corner. After a one-hour flight from Dàlián to Seoul, a seven-hour layover in Seoul, a four-and-a-half-hour flight to Cebu, Philippines, an overnight stay in what I must claim as the nastiest hotel room in which I have ever stayed, another one-hour flight to Kalibo, Philippines, a two-hour drive on winding roads through abject poverty which I later learned was common to most Filipinos, a 15-minute boat ride, and then a 15-minute drive in a tuk-tuk, one would think we traveled to the edge of the earth. Instead, me and a few expat friends landed at the doorstep of 357 Boracay,[35] our most excellent beachside hotel on the White Sand Beach of Boracay (pronounced "bor-OCK-kai"), a sand speck of an island among the 7,107 that the Philippines has to offer. For a place that was difficult to reach, I was somewhat surprised by the diversity of the foreigners who also found the place. There were the European expats from China, Europeans from Europe; other Americans from China (Běijīng, Guǎngzhōu, and Shēnzhèn (深圳)) making the Golden Week escape; Chinese from China and Hong Kong doing the same; Singaporeans, Koreans, more Germans than some German villages; and, of course, the Australians who have the best understanding of "extended vacation" in the world.

In Boracay, the world revolves around diving, drinking, dancing, and days on end of lying on the beach under the hot sun. A vacation destination not only for foreigners, but also for Filipinos, Boracay is a place to go when you want to have a good time and to forget about life for a while. The local population — friendly, quick with a smile, with a keen sense of customer service and always happy to help a wayward tourist — gives the tourist areas of Boracay a warm vibe second only to the warm tropical breezes. What it does not revolve around is driving, since the main thoroughfare is a sandy footpath about a mile long, 20 feet wide, and lined with dive shops, trinket shops, hotels, bars, restaurants, and the occasional massage parlor. But like any other

35 http://www.357boracay.com/

tourist destination where wealth is concentrated along the beach — Atlantic City, New Jersey; Ipanema Beach, Brazil; Nassau, Bahamas; the Dominican Republic come to mind — it's not wise for the random tourist to wander very far from the beach. Wander too far, and you or your money just might not make it back.

Boracay was postcard perfect with its sandy beach lined with palm trees waving in the sea breeze, warm turquoise waters, and more nubile Filipinas in various flavors of hotness and cuteness (bikinis, miniskirts, hot pants, skimpy whatever) than one could shake their stick at. At first I thought I found Paradise Island, but when a Filipino midget called me "Boss", I realized I might have landed on Fantasy Island instead. I'm almost positive that typhoons were the furthest thing from Chairman Mao's mind when he formed the People's Republic of China on October 1, 1949, but this Chinese Golden Week occurs when typhoons are most prevalent in the Southwestern Pacific. True to form, it rained every day in Boracay because Super Typhoon Krosa, just to the northeast of us, was giving Taiwan a much-needed scrubbing. As long as there was a ready supply of cold San Miguel, the rain and the occasional power outages were just a minor nuisance. The beaches in Boracay during the low season were peacefully empty, which was a refreshing change from China. A few of the foreigners who took up residence in Boracay suggested that we consider a return trip during peak season because that's when the seas were at their calmest, the beach its whitest, and the sky its bluest. When I raised the concern about Boracay being asses-to-elbows during the peak season, the response I received was, "but all those asses belong to bikini clad Filipinas…"

As single white guys in Boracay, my friends and I regularly found us to be the objects of many slow, deliberate, and intense head-to-toe-toe-to-head scans by the Filipinas. For the girls walking in groups, we would usually get the laser beam stare and the eventual over the shoulder double take from most of them after we passed. As for the girls who were looking to trade up from the Western boyfriend with whom they walked arm-in-arm, the modus operandi was the same minus the double-take. I'm sure no love would be lost if those couples split up, because each would be flying solo for only a day or two, at most. I met one 19-year-old Filipina whose German boyfriend kicked her out of his apartment. A day or so after they broke up, when he showed up at her place of work with his new Filipina girlfriend to ask her when she was going to remove her stuff from his apartment, the German found her in the arms of another Western guy. One management professor friend of mine calls this the "Dixie Cup Effect": take one and throw it away, and another will immediately take its place.

There are those who move to the Philippines because they gave up on, and checked out of, the Western World. There are others who are there because they found their own tropical paradise, a slower pace to life, and a very low cost of living in the company of those ubiquitous 18-to-20-something Filipinas. One word of caution: those Filipinas may be just a bit much for the aged man. One of my friends met a 20-year-old Filipina widow and mother of a 2-year-old whose German husband died of a heart attack. Besides those Western men who found their Miss Right, there were also many who gave new meaning to the phrase "embracing the local culture" when they paired up with Miss Right Now. One night, I met a Danish guy with a Filipina under his arm who told me he had been in Hong Kong on business and he decided to hop over to Boracay while his wife opted to stay in Hong Kong. But sometimes ignorance is bliss, and people in Boracay generally don't ask a lot of questions of others. Like Phuket, Thailand, it's part of what makes Boracay a tropical paradise.

"Dave", a relatively fit, early forty-something Australian moved to Boracay in 2005 and became a resident. For those interested, a two-year temporary residence permit for the Philippines is a mere $400 plus $250 for a two-year extension; or if you decide to marry a Filipina, a permanent residence visa costs about $500.[36]

36 http://www.living-in-the-philippines.com/permanent-resident-visa-philippines.shtml

He told me that he lived comfortably in Boracay on the interest earned by his savings account back home. He said that the most expensive part of living in Boracay was housing, so he bought some land and in 2007 was building a place to live and apartments to sell or rent. As for food and drink, a stuffed-to-gills dinner out cost about $15 per person, a beer at a bar went for about $1.00, while top-shelf mixed drinks will max out at $10 each. If Dave wanted to eat at home, he said he could buy a couple pounds of fresh oysters for just $0.35. Then again, he didn't have to do any of the shopping because he left that up to his 22-year-old Filipina girlfriend. Not only did she do the shopping, she also cooked, cleaned, sewed buttons back onto his shirts, and gave him massages, manicures and pedicures. But what Dave found most interesting was that his girlfriend never asked for anything. As a girl "from the provinces", he said, she had never seen a plasma screen TV, or had a hot shower[37] until she moved into Dave's apartment, and, Dave made a point to emphasize, her own bedroom.

Dave was the second Western man in as many days who told me that his Filipino girlfriend didn't ask for anything, even though the Western men could and would probably have provided whatever the girls requested. Those two guys, by the way, didn't seem too disappointed with being with low maintenance girls. By not asking for anything, it seemed that the girls were trying their best to not be burdensome lest they cause their boyfriend to invoke the Dixie Cup Effect. Mix the widespread poverty beyond the beach and throughout the rest of the Philippines with the mon-eyed, transient population of a tourist destination, and it is not hard to imagine that the girls are hoping on the Law of Probability by giving what they got to the continuous stream of random guys who show an interest. As the theory goes, if one plays the Powerball Lottery enough times, they will eventually hit the jackpot. The girls never have to worry about the infinite flow of men drying

---

37   Many provincial Filipino homes do not have hot water since it's just too damn hot to shower in hot water.

up because there is always plenty of interest among Western men for Filipinas, albeit the goals and expectations of each participant in the relationship may not necessarily be aligned.

After a week in Boracay, I was ready to head back to Dàlián. It wasn't because I was getting tired of window shopping, too tired of mellowing out with a book or magazine, too tired of walking along the beach, or too tired of paying rock bottom prices for good food and stiff drinks. Rather, staying any longer than a week would have ruined the vacation feel of Boracay because I would have had to start doing mundane things like laundry and shopping. I also didn't want to stay there long enough for the island to lose its mystique as the tropical paradise seen on the postcards.

Then again, I was probably there too long already. Near the end of the trip, I realized that "Boracay" is really Tagalog for "broken glass" because I had never seen another beach in the world, outside of China, so badly polluted with it. The only saving grace was that the glass in Boracay is known as "sea glass" and had all its sharp edges sanded smooth. Boracay also has a large canine population that roams free along the beach, urinating on seaweed, tables, chairs, life jackets, and whatever else looks like a good target. When the dogs were not urinating, they were sleeping, eating, or humping. But the dogs were only a minor nuisance that a couple good Korean restaurants could fix in a jiffy. As for all those pretty girls, if something is too good to be true, then it probably is: some of those Filipina hotties pee standing up. While out one night, I heard a story from a British woman whose friend's friend picked up a Filipina one night in one of the island's most popular dance clubs. When they eventually found themselves back in his room, the girl tied the man to his bed and left him there to be raped by her lady-boy friend who followed them.

Rain and all, the 2007 trek to Boracay was worthwhile, and Boracay will go onto the list of possible places I'd consider if, just in case, I wanted or needed to go into hiding. Even more so now in 2012 now that several five-star hotels, beach clubs and resorts have opened; there still remain plenty of restaurants serving fresh and inexpensive seafood; and the many bars along the beach provide many opportunities for people to while away the tropical days chatting with old friends or new acquaintances. I can only hope that Boracay does not join Dahab, Egypt; the SAS Radisson in Amman, Jordan; the Taba Hilton in Taba, Egypt; Nuweiba, Egypt; Eilat, Israel; Jerusalem; Kuta Beach, Bali; and the World Trade Center on my other list, which is that of all the destinations bombed by terrorists once I visited them.

CHAPTER 10

PATIENCE IS A PARADOX

IN 2007 WHEN FRIENDS AND FAMILY VISITED ME IN SHÀNGHĂI, MOST returned home realizing that China had an amazing buzz and energy that is no longer seen in the United States. China hums with a ubiquitous frenetic energy and enthusiasm as millions of people do a lot of hustling, bustling, pushing and shoving to get their share of the pie as if someone's about ready to scream "Last Call!" forever. But with all that hustling and bustling comes one of the greatest mysteries in the world: the Chinese Patience Paradox, which requires everyone in China to demonstrate a high degree of patience to overcome an unintended and undesired situation caused by the same exact population that also demonstrates a high degree of impatience.

In my travels, I saw many examples of people trying to wring every last second of waiting out of their day for some perceived but seemingly ever elusive gain. I met many college-educated Chinese who could only shake their head in frustration and talk about the impatience of "the Chinese people" in the third person while they themselves were frantically pushing the "Door Close" button to save an extra few seconds in an elevator, even if the elevator doors were in mid-amputation of some poor soul who wasn't quick enough for the button-pusher. Unstated Chinese elevator etiquette requires the person closest to the button panel to push the "Door Close" button to speed things up, but whenever I held the coveted position I would just stand there waiting for the doors to close. I would relish those few seconds that were an eternity to the passengers because Chinese Water Torture – or water-boarding for that matter – is child's play compared to Chinese Elevator Torture.

Second to the elevator, my favorite Patience Paradox prop is the motorized revolving door. It all starts with a crowd of Chinese people crushing into a revolving door to the point where it resembles a glass sardine can. Once everyone is packed tight and people are shuffling an inch at a time to the outdoors as the door rotates, there was always that one last person who wants to jump in just before the door closes on them rather than waiting a few more seconds for the empty door to come back around. This causes the safety sensors in the door to stop the motor for a few seconds so the offending person doesn't lose an appendage. Those precious few seconds that now feel like an eternity from inside the door – especially during the summer months – are now lost to those whose day briefly comes to a screeching halt. One person tries to save three seconds, but wastes another five seconds for themselves and each of the other dozen or so people stuck in the door. Maybe the safety features should be disabled so Darwinism can take over.

Human impatience has been studied and defined and redefined over the last hundred years. It's been reported[38] that impatience was a result of "incompleteness of the imagination" and a "defect in will" or a "faulty telescopic faculty". Although not yet formally studied, a typical day in China shows that impatience takes over the regions of the brain responsible for logic and strategy, leaving an offending person farther behind when compared to the original situation they tried to expedite. During a trip out of the Dàlián International Airport, I was about the eighth person in the security line when another security counter opened up next to my

---

38   Bommier, A., "Irrational Impatience?", *Toulouse School of Economics (CNRS, GREMAQ)*, April 11, 2008.

line. Some of the seven people in front of me and several others from other lines sprinted over to the newly-opened counter with their carry-on luggage in tow in hopes of taking the pole position. The woman who was originally in front of me was now the eighth person in her new line while I simply stepped forward in my line to occupy the third spot. When I was through security and on my way to my gate, she was still fifth in line.

There are several Chinese proverbs, such as "A hasty man drinks his tea with a fork", to espouse the negative impacts of impatience, but unfortunately none of them involve cars and drivers. It's on the highways where patience is required the most and where the Chinese people should heed the Chinese proverb which warns, "If you are patient in a time of anger, you will escape a hundred days of sorrow." In Dàlián, it is not uncommon for drivers to use one of the oncoming lanes as a new lane when the lane they are driving in becomes clogged with traffic. On more than one occasion I watched the rush-hour traffic morph from two lanes in each direction into three lanes in one direction and one in the opposite direction because people did not want to wait in traffic any longer. I'm sure if there were more cars going in the predominant direction, the road would have easily become an ad hoc one-way street. Vehicular traffic is the most obvious example of the Patience Paradox because everything is go-go-go until an accident turns it into stop-stop-stop, traffic backs up for miles, the police are called, and before anyone knows, all the perceived money and time saved or earned from rushing around has simply evaporated into a deficit. According to a 2004 study by the Medical School of Jìnán University (暨南大学) in Guǎngzhōu, China, the direct economic losses from traffic accidents was estimated at 3.3 billion RMB, or $397 million at the time of the study.[39] According to a 2004 World Health Organization report, road traffic injuries in China in 1999 resulted in a cumulative loss of

---

39 http://www.chinadaily.com.cn/english/doc/2004-04/12/content_322695.htm

12.6 million "potentially productive life years."[40] In August 2008, the World Bank issued a working paper[41] stating that road traffic incidents cost China approximately 0.4% of GDP, which is a third the GDP loss estimated by the World Health Organization, which put losses between 1-1.5 percent GDP.[42] In dollar terms, the 2010 Chinese GDP came in at $6.04 trillion, about a 10 percent rise over 2009. Doing a little math on the low-end estimate, a 0.4 percent loss of GDP may seem small, but turns out to be about $21.8 billion in lost productivity while the high-end estimate calculates out to some $82 billion in lost productivity in 2010 attributed to injuries and deaths from car accidents alone.

One can only imagine the GDP losses from non-traffic related incidents given that, in 2010, car ownership in China was on par with the U.S. prior to World War II. The Chinese regularly shortcut safety precautions for convenience or to save themselves time and money. It's not uncommon to drive past a construction site and see workers dozens of stories above the ground working without safety belts and harnesses. One American friend of mine in the construction industry told me that on his very first trip to China in 2005, he looked out his Chéngdū (成都) hotel window and watched a worker fall to his death at a neighboring construction site. He then watched the man's coworkers drag the body to the edge of the construction site before returning to work. By the time my friend returned to his hotel at the end of the day, the body was gone. While working in China, I spent the better portion of my time on a construction site reminding dozens of workers each day to wear their fall protection or their safety glasses. Each time I

40   "World Report on Road Traffic Injury Prevention", the World Health Organization, 2004. http://www.who.int/violence_injury_prevention/publications/road_traffic/world_report/summary_en_rev.pdf
41   "China Road Traffic Safety: The Achievements, the Challenges, and the Way Ahead," World Bank, August 2008.
42   "World Report on Road Traffic Injury Prevention", the World Health Organization, 2004. http://www.who.int/violence_injury_prevention/publications/road_traffic/world_report/summary_en_rev.pdf

asked them why they didn't like to wear their gear they all told me that it wasn't convenient and that it hindered their productivity, as if falling to their death or going blind was a lesser concern. I'm positive none of those guys realized that, according to the Chinese government official statistics, workplace deaths in 2006 chipped two percent, or $54 billion off the GDP.[43]

To better understand why the Chinese shortcut safety and risk life and limb for productivity, I liked to press my Chinese friends with what turned out to be uncomfortable questions for them. I would always start off with softball questions to get them talking so they didn't realize what was happening until it happened. It was easy to tell when the Chinese reached the end of their comfort zone because my questions were suddenly followed by a pregnant pause, maybe a slight chuckle, and a terse response that could

43   http://www.gov.cn/english/2006-03/07/content_220591.htm

easily be translated into no response. When I asked my friend Sophia about why the Chinese are always in a rush, she thought about it for a few seconds and then gave me an "I don't know", as in "I don't know what you're talking about." I knew she knew what I was talking about because she had spent her university years in Dublin, Ireland. I then gave her a real-time example by pointing to the car in front of us that was using the shoulder of the road as a passing lane, and my own driver who just cut off a half dozen cars by using the empty left turn lane as a shortcut to drive straight. After another pregnant pause, she finally said, "because they want to make more money." When I asked another Chinese friend the same question, she paused for a moment and then gave me an answer that could be summarized as, "old habits die hard."

Besides the lady at the security line at the Dàlián airport, air travel is also rife with examples supporting the existence of the Patience Paradox. As soon as the first rear wheel of a plane hits the ground, there's always a chorus of clicks from everyone undoing their seatbelt in relief as if the belts were two sizes too small. When the plane is just off the runway and taxiing to the gate, some people feel the need to get up to fetch their things from the overhead bin, causing the flight attendants to scramble up to direct the rule-breakers back to their seats. Before the plane is stopped at the gate, everyone in the back rows pushes through those in front of them who are still trying to retrieve their belongings from the overhead bins and toward a still-closed door. I'm not sure how any of this rushing around is earning anyone more money. The irony of it all is that all this impatience only extends the waiting time – and reinforces the need for more patience – at the baggage carousel for everyone who checked their luggage. One Chinese friend told me about his fellow countrymen during a flight from Hong Kong to Mainland China: when flying out of Hong Kong, the mainland Chinese entered the plane in an orderly manner like the Hong Kong residents. However when the plane landed in mainland China, all of the previously-orderly

Mainlanders reverted back to their old ways as if was expected of them. As they say, "When in Rome…"

But some of the Romans are not too appreciative when foreigners try to do as they do. As we were taxiing to the gate after one flight from Dàlián to Běijīng, I mentally prepared myself for the disembarking ritual. After the plane stopped, I stood up into an already jammed aisle with me separating 30-something rows of people from the door. To keep from being plowed over by the press of humanity, I made a large presence in the aisle with a few nudges to those who were already pressing up against and nudging me. My attempt to make space was not looked too kindly upon by one fellow traveler who was pressed up against me, and he started yelling at me in Chinese. I was now the Ugly White Boy for following the crowd. I don't know what he had to say, but I know he wasn't happy since he continued to yell at me as we were in the jet way and then again in the airport on the way to baggage claim. I guess extreme individualism is acceptable in China only if it's practiced by the Chinese. The rest of us need to follow the rules.

It's easy to understand how individuals who are focused on looking out for themselves (the button-pusher in the elevator or the wrong-way driver) can step on the feet of others (the potential amputee or head-on collision victim), but there must be more to the whole patience paradox since all the rushing around, in the big scheme of things, removes money from people's pockets and value from their lives. Around 190 B.C., Jewish scholar Jesus Ben Sirach wrote, "There is one that toileth and laboureth, and maketh haste, and is so much the more behind", which was later popularized by Ben Franklin in the *Poor Richard's Almanac* as simply "haste makes waste". Both these instances in history were lost on the Chinese because of simple logistics and a lack of high-speed telecommunications, but it seems that some behaviors are common across all people and all societies. Confucius, who was Chinese through and through, wasn't far off the mark when he said, "Do not make haste, and do not desire petty gains. If you make haste you will miss your goal; if you covet petty gains, you will fail in bigger and more important affairs." Confucius also is attributed with saying "haste brings no success; haste makes waste; more haste, less speed." ("无欲速, 无见小利. 欲速则不达, 见小利则大事不成也"). But Confucius was also considered by some to be a country bumpkin from the still-rural backwater of Qūfù (曲阜) in a remote part of Shāndōng (山东) Province, and anyone from rural America knows how much respect they get from their urban cousins.

The Ying and Yang of the Patience Paradox has been around for a very long time. At least as far back in time as the creation of the Chinese language, that is. One Chinese word for "patience" is *nài xīn* (耐心) where *nài* (耐) means "resistance" and *xīn* (心) means "heart", since patience requires a strong/durable/resistant heart to not lash out against the selfish and impatient. Another translation for "patience" is *rěn* (忍) which has a meaning closer to "endure". The top part of the character "忍", 刃 (*rèn*) is the character for "knife edge", and the bottom part of "忍" is "heart"; for sometimes it takes strength to endure a knife on the heart, a stopped revolving door, or an elevator door that just won't close. No one should seem surprised that Chinese patience involves both hearts and daggers. But what is lost on many non-Chinese speakers is that the word for "patience/endurance" is *rěn*; that for knife edge is *rèn*; while that for "people" is *rén*. Go figure.

CHAPTER 11

MAKIN' LEMONADE

MANAGEMENT SCHOOLS AND BUSINESS JOURNALS LIKE TO TALK ABOUT turning lemons into lemonade, an analogy for how leaders find and exploit opportunities in otherwise bad situations. If the business schools or economically depressed municipalities across America are looking for a great example of how to make some lemonade, they should consider a trip to Hā'ěrbīn (哈尔滨). Hā'ěrbīn is the northernmost major city in China, located in Hēilóngjiāng (黑龙江) Province about two hundred miles from of the Russian border and a 90-minute flight north of Dàlián. That means Hā'ěrbīn and its 3.1 million people along the mile-wide Sōnghuā (松花) River are a hop, skip, and a jump from Siberia, and we all know what's in Siberia...

On a January 2008 business trip to Shànghǎi, the day before my flight to Hā'ěrbīn, I saw a billboard advertising Hēilóngjiāng Province and Hā'ěrbīn as a summer destination for great hikes, blue skies, fishing, camping and lakeside beaches. There was nothing really advertising Hā'ěrbīn as a winter destination, which made me wonder about the decision making process my coworkers and I used prior to booking our trip. If the arctic temperatures and barren landscape were not enough to entice visitors, Hā'ěrbīn's tourism board could always count on one of the area's most famous tourist attractions to rake them in: Unit

731, the Japanese Germ Warfare testing laboratory[44] that claimed the lives of hundreds of thousands of Chinese, Soviet, Korean, British, American, and other prisoners of war during World War II. I don't know if this was the reason for the several pharmaceutical companies I saw or read about during my weekend in Hā'ĕrbīn, but when a germ warfare testing center is considered a primary tourist attraction, it's not hard to see that the mayor of Hā'ĕrbīn was facing down a mountain of lemons. But as it turns out, Hā'ĕrbīn is an excellent example how some resourceful and innovative Chinese leaders made the most of what they had available – snow for five months of the year and an unlimited supply of ice – and turned it into money with the Harbin International Ice and Snow Sculpture Festival Hā'ĕrbīn Guójì Bīngxuĕ Jié, 哈尔滨国际冰雪节), held each January and February.

---

44   http://www.kimsoft.com/korea/jp-germ.htm

The snow and ice festival has been a Chinese tradition since 1965 and later again in 1985 after a brief hiatus during the Cultural Revolution, but it wasn't until 1999 when someone decided to power up Hā'ěrbīn's monster lemonade machine to make the city a world-famous international destination modeled on the annual Chinese Ice Lantern Festival that started during the Qing Dynasty (1644-1911). Back in the day, local peasants and fishermen used ice lanterns to protect their candles from the Siberian winds. The lanterns were made by filling a bucket with water, and putting it outdoors to freeze. Ice would form first on the bucket walls and grow inwards. Once the ice was thick enough to stand on its own, the remaining water was emptied from the bucket, the ice was removed, turned upside-down, and a hole was made in the top of the ice to let in oxygen. When placed over a candle the ice would not only protect the flame from the winds but would magnify the light of the candle. These days, hundreds of thousands of visitors from around China and the world brave the shortened days and the subzero temperatures to watch artists create ice and snow sculptures that somehow defy the laws of gravity.

Visiting the snow sculpture park to see a childhood activity taken to an entirely new order of magnitude and level of complexity will cost each person 120 RMB (about $18). The orange tint from the midday sun that makes the whole day feel like a late afternoon gives the sculptures more depth and color and less of the obnoxious glare that can lead to snow blindness and bad photos. After sundown, a visit to the mother of all ice displays will cost another 150RMB (about $22) and a few broken bones if not careful navigating the hundreds of stairs, sans handrails, made from blocks of ice. Neither of these venues are cheap by Chinese standards, but Hā'ěrbīn is a very popular destination among Chinese tourists. Money aside, both these displays are well worth the frostbitten toes and fingers. The price of admission to the displays is a minor contributor to the local economy while the real money goes to the hotels, restaurants, tour companies, and airlines. If you're planning a trip, you better book your hotel early otherwise you might be, quite literally, left out in the cold. During the festival weekends, even the $200/night five-star hotels are fully booked with foreign tourists, expats, and the wealthy Chinese. One European man I chatted with in my hotel elevator was in Hā'ěrbīn with his coworkers from Shànghǎi for a corporate team-building event. He talked about the weekend as if he were in St. Moritz, which tells me that not many people these days take note of the WWII relic out on the south side of town.

Besides the snow and ice sculptures, one can stroll along the chilly Zhōng Yāng Dà Jiē (中央大街) which is advertised by the Hā'ěrbīn tourism board as the longest shopping pedestrian street in Asia. In addition to fake furs, fake Rolexes, dozens of types and flavors of Russian vodka and just about as many flavors of Russian chocolate (there's a reason Russian chocolate isn't famous), there are some fine examples of Russian architecture from the early 20th century when Russia ruled that particular roost. To complete a weekend in Hā'ěrbīn, it's worth making a stop by St. Sophia's Cathedral with its telltale Russian Orthodox onion dome, but don't get your hopes up too high if you're expecting the inside to reflect the outside. Also make sure you book a Sunday afternoon flight out of Hā'ěrbīn so you can use the morning to hop over to the Siberian Tiger Park, not far from the ice sculpture park, where the tigers run wild and visitors caged in buses can buy live chickens, goats, and cows to feed to the tigers, National Geographic style. While waiting for your flight don't miss the chance to snack on some of the best locally-made smoked sausage east of Moscow, topped off with a Qingdao beer from one of the convenience stores.

By swapping out the germ warfare laboratory for a more wholesome government project (the St. Lawrence Seaway) and reducing the population by 3,090,000, this frozen Chinese city reminded me of my hometown of Massena: one big river, a whole lot of ice, snow, cold, and empty land, all located near an international border. Maybe it is because Hā'ĕrbīn (Latitude: 45° 45' 0" N, Longitude: 126° 39' 0" E) and Massena (Latitude: 44° 55' 49" N, Longitude: 74° 53' 27" W), share the same gray, leafless trees and bitter cold, sunny days that are familiar to northeastern winters along the 45th parallel. Hā'ĕrbīn clearly benefits from all the frenetic rushing around characteristic of many Chinese cities but I couldn't help but wonder why Hā'ĕrbīn is more prosperous than Massena.

Massena, after all, is first place in the world where, in 1902, aluminum smelting became economically feasible on an industrial scale. It was there that the Aluminum Company of America (ALCOA) opened their first factory which now holds the record for being the longest operating aluminum smelter in the U.S. By 1917, over 50 languages were spoken in Massena, and Massena was cosmopolitan before its time. But today, if I was ever unfortunate enough to be diagnosed with a terminal disease and given only six months to live, I'd move back to Massena because those six months would seem like an eternity. Why is communist Hā'ĕrbīn more prosperous than a democratic, capitalist, and declining Massena? In Hā'ĕrbīn, people took action, made investments, and figured things out. In Massena and in many other local municipalities across the country, there seems to be more people who do a lot of talking than there are people who do a lot of walking. The talkers are usually the Jill and Joe Sixpacks complaining about how they can't pay their subprime mortgages because the Chinese and Indians stole their minimum wage jobs; or government leaders who allow themselves to be hindered by special interests or by avoiding the painfully inconvenient but necessary long-term solutions that, yes, may not get them reelected, but are the right things for the community. Everyone is always looking to hit home runs with major projects rather than win the game the hard way through a bunch of base runs. That is, if they get that far because it's always easier for those in charge to say "no" than to embrace possibility thinking reminiscent of the early days of the U.S. space program or the St. Lawrence Seaway.

Saying "no" is the easy way out; saying "yes" means that some hard work and risk taking needs to happen. The elected forget that they need to put forth effort and resources to reap the benefits of investment. Money needs to be spent for it to be made.

George Washington Carver said, "Ninety-nine percent of failures come from people who have the habit of making excuses." If cavemen were able to sustain the human race with less education and resources than the average American, then one would think that Americans would be able figure out a plan to make some lemonade. Instead, the local and national economies remain in the toilet because no one wants to make the sacrifices inherent with compromise. Then again, maybe no one wants to get their hands dirty. When George W. Bush was president, he proposed an immigration bill to allow illegal immigrants to remain in the U.S. to do the jobs that Americans wouldn't do. That there are jobs that Americans won't do in an economy with a sustained unemployment rate hovering around eight percent after the Great Recession is a testament to the co-opting of the Protestant Work Ethic and American Dream that made the U.S. a singular global powerhouse. Thomas Edison proclaimed, "Opportunity is missed by most people because it is dressed in overalls and looks like work." Has America become so soft and arrogant with its sense of entitlement that even the president of a country founded on elbow grease thinks that some jobs are too dirty for Americans to perform? This is clearly divergent from another Republican president, Calvin Coolidge, who said, "All growth depends upon activity. There is no development physically or intellectually without effort, and effort means work." Unfortunately, it seems the American Empire has become fat, dumb, lazy, and oblivious to, literally, the billions of people around the world who get their hands dirty every day. In China alone, there are more manual laborers earning, on average, $1.00 per hour than there are Americans. Many of them are working hundreds of miles away from families they might see only one week each year, if they survive to make it home at all. I have seen, talked to, and watched some of those Chinese laborers up close, and I can honestly say that even the Mexicans should fear for their jobs. Come to think of it, they may be too late: I found a Chinese restaurant in Phoenix, Arizona owned and operated by the native Chinese that employs one Hispanic waitress.

In the case of Hā'ĕrbīn, it was creativity that went hand in hand with hard work that fostered the international reputation of the ice festival. Although international teams pay an entry fee to compete in the snow sculpture contest, some of the larger snow and ice displays were provided by local labor. The first prize in the competition is only a couple hundred dollars, so almost all the money stays locally. What's even cooler is that making ice and snow sculptures is an environmentally-sustainable activity. The snow and ice are, for the time being, renewable and local natural resources. It's hard to not be impressed by the Hā'ĕrbīn ice and snow festival. It's not every day a city can transform itself from being a germ warfare capital of the world to the ice and snow sculpture capital of the world. Google "Harbin Ice Festival" and see what you find. The leadership in Hā'ĕrbīn has done a fine job in making this transition, and they are a model to other communities looking to spice up their economies on the cheap with environmentally-sustainable activities.

Then again, maybe the economy is too spicy. Even Hā'ĕrbīn's cabbies were getting in on the action, but they were squeezing more than lemons. Where Dàlián could be a contender for having some of the most dangerous cabbies and traffic in China, Hā'ĕrbīn is in the running as the city with the most blatantly dishonest cabbies. Being ripped off by the first Hā'ĕrbīn resident we met set a negative tone for our entire visit. Of the 13 of us who traveled to Hā'ĕrbīn that one weekend, we had more bad taxi experiences than good. For those going to Hā'ĕrbīn, it costs about 120 RMB ($16.22 at the time) from the airport to downtown, not the 150RMB, 200RMB, and 340RMB ($20.27, $27.03, and $45.95, respectively) that my coworkers and I were charged by our cabbies. Stick with the newer-looking green-and-white taxis and never, ever, ever, get into a red taxi unless you absolutely, positively need to do so. On the way back to the airport, I told the driver of our green-and-white taxi about our taxi experiences and he immediately made a phone call and gave us the phone number for the traffic bureau so we could file a complaint. If being overcharged by the cabbies was not enough, it seemed common practice by all cabbies to charge an additional 1 RMB ($0.16) above the metered rate. I asked one coworker about the charge and he said it was a fuel surcharge, which seemed suspicious since cabbies in Shànghǎi, Běijīng, and Dàlián at the time didn't take extra money without it being offered. In the end, it appeared that this surcharge was just a tip to which they thought they were entitled to for doing their regular job. My tip for struggling American towns and cities is to look at Hā'ěrbīn, Dàlián, and other developing Chinese cities for pointers on to how to make good out of a bad situation. As for the cabbies, the only tip that I'll be handing out to them if I return to Hā'ěrbīn will be, "你应该不吃黄色的雪" or "*Ní yīng gāi bù chī huáng se de xuě*", better known to us English speakers as "You shouldn't eat yellow snow."

CHAPTER 12

JESUS, DRAGONS, AND GROUNDHOGS....OH MY!

IN EARLY 2008, DÀLIÁN WAS IN THE MIDST OF A BITTER COLD AND windy Manchurian winter. I was getting tired of bundling up as if I was going on a moonwalk each time I left my apartment. That March, I found myself in Běijīng visiting with my friend Julian from the U.S. who was in China on business. But instead of facing down another Siberian Express, it was sunny and 60 degrees. Plum blossoms were in bloom and buds were starting to form on trees. While walking around the Forbidden City, the Temple of Heaven, the Lama Temple, and what remains of the traditional Chinese neighbors known as the Běijīng Hutongs, we even started to work up a sweat. What a difference it made to be inland. Spring, and some smog were in the Běijīng air, and that only meant one thing: spring was on its way to Dàlián.

While on the way back to my apartment after my flight landed at the Dàlián airport that Sunday evening, I saw some fireworks in the sky. The Chinese use fireworks to celebrate weddings, opening new businesses, funerals, the Lunar New Year, etc., but 8:30 p.m. on Sunday, March 9, 2008, seemed like an odd time to be lighting up the sky. I asked Wáng about the celebratory mood, and he said that it was *Zhōng Hé Jié* (中和节). The *Zhōng Hé* Festival is said to celebrate the time when hibernating insects wake up at the start of spring as the weather starts to warm up. With the insects waking up, another ancient practice during the *Zhōng Hé* Festival was to fumigate homes by burning various herbs and incense. If someone was trying to fumigate Dàlián with their fireworks that evening, they should have had a bigger bomb.

Zhōng Hé Jié is also known as *Lóng Tái Tóu* (龙抬头), or "Dragon Raising its Head" because the dragon, who fiddles with the weather and is the bringer of the rains that revive the insects, is said to raise its head to make sure that things are still in order. While some of Dàlián's residents were trying to initiate some urban renewal that evening with their leftover New Year's fireworks, most people celebrate *Lóng Tái Tóu* by getting their hair cut. It's believed that a haircut on this day – the first haircut since the beginning of the new lunar year – brings good luck because they want to raise their head like the dragon, the symbol of wisdom, good fortune, and strength. What better way to show off their best than with a new haircut? People want to raise their head just like the dragon, and to make things easier, they go for a haircut to make their head weigh less, or so goes the thinking of some. Honestly, if someone needs to rely on a haircut to make their head light enough to lift, they're going to need all the good luck they can find as well as a gym membership. It was my good fortune to get my hair cut the weekend prior because I was able to avoid the crowds of people at the local hair shop with their dark clouds of bad luck in tow. Even the Chinese legends allow flexibility for the sake of convenience: for those who don't have time to go for a haircut, they can wash their hair instead to get the same effect, which begs the question whether or not this would be someone's first hair wash of the new Lunar New Year. For those who don't have hair, they can eat noodles or pancakes on this day to bring them luck, furthering the need for the gym membership. But be warned – don't do any sewing or expect to get any clothes mended on this day lest the needle poke out the dragon's eye and ruin the holiday for everyone.

The kicker here is that Dragon Raising Its Head Day, Haircut Day, No Sewing Day, Hair Wash Day, Pancake Day, Incense Day, or whatever you want to call it, is always celebrated on the second day of the second month of the lunar calendar. The day most of the world knew as February 7, 2008, was January 1, 2008 of the Chinese Lunar calendar, which meant that March 9, 2008, of the solar calendar was February 2, 2008, on the Chinese Lunar calendar, making March 9, 2008, the Lunar Groundhog's Day. Who thought Groundhog's Day déjà vu was only limited to the Bill Murray movie?

For those who want to experience more than their fair share of Americana, head to Punxsutawney, Pennsylvania on the solar February 2. If Punxsutawney Phil, America's official groundhog, sees his shadow, then there will be another six weeks of winter. This, in itself, makes no sense because if Phil sees his shadow, then the sun must be shining. As the story goes, the guy in Punxsutawney who understands groundhog-speak receives a report from Phil about whether or not there will be six more weeks of winter. Of course, how does Phil send the report about seeing his shadow if his shadow scared him back into his hole? Then again, if you count the number of days from February 2, 2008, to the spring equinox – the official first day of spring when the earth is nearly vertical with respect to the sun and when the durations for day and night are the same – you'll find that there will always be about six weeks until spring. So, the whole Punxsutawney Groundhog thing appears to be a tourist event cooked up by the Punxsutawney Chamber of Commerce for those who can't read a calendar or haven't studied astronomy. Maybe Hā'ěrbīn's leaders took a few pointers from Punxsutawney's founding fathers responsible for firing up their lemonade machine.

Although the symbolism of *Lóng Tái Tóu* and Groundhog's Day are somewhat similar, that's about where the similarities end. The solar date for *Lóng Tái Tóu* changes each year because it is dependent on the Chinese Lunar New Year, which is, depending on the year, the day of the second or third new moon after the winter solstice. Groundhog's Day has its origins as the pagan Celtic celebration Imbolc,[45] a feast day that centers on fertility rites and forecasting the weather, which sits midway between the winter and spring solstices and is celebrated on February 1. If a night out at Copper Faced Jacks in Dublin is any indication, the Celts are still doing a fine job keeping up with fertility traditions, but I never saw a groundhog in Ireland during the year I lived and worked there. So, the correlation of Lóng Tái Tóu with Groundhog's Day is some sort of funky lunar-solar celestial convergence type of coincidence. The only thing the Chinese and early Irish had in common was agriculture and the tendency to watch the sun, moon, and stars. We must be impressed, though, on the ability of these distant cultures to come up with the same conclusions from reading the stars – or is there a yet-undiscovered connection between the Chinese and the Celts? These days a northbound stroll along O'Connell Street in Dublin starting at the Stiffy on the Liffey[46] shows that the Irish and the Chinese have a bit more in common, specifically the entire neighborhood at the north end of O'Connell Street. One exasperated Dublin cabbie told me in September 2010, "At first, the Chinese were no problem. They kept to themselves." But now, he said, "they're starting to sprout wings…." To both our dismay, he said that the Chinese were starting to become cabbies.

Pagans being pagans, it's safe to assume that they did their fair share of carousing, and it should be no surprise that the early Romans also had their own pagan purification ritual that took place every year in early February. Given that several of today's Western societies evolved from the Romans who raped and plundered their way through Europe, it's plausible that the Romans were responsible for perpetuating the whole groundhog

45 http://landscaping.about.com/cs/pestcontrol/a/groundhog_day_4.htm
46 The Dublin Spire, along the River Liffey, that some regard as a phallic symbol, albeit a pointy, skinny one.

celebration. The only catch was that groundhogs were not native to Rome, and they used hedgehogs instead. Sunshine is native to Rome, but the Romans checked to see if the hedgehog saw its shadow on clear, moonlit nights.[47]

The Chinese have trumped the Western world on this one, if only for the fact that the Chinese are using a dragon as their symbol. Would you rather celebrate February 2 with a macho dragon or a furry critter that lives in a hole in the ground? In contrast to the Western version of the evil fire-breathing dragon that had to be slayed, the Chinese dragon is an all-powerful myth-ical creature considered to be a potent symbol of luck, fortune, and power — think Bruce Lee, who is known to the Chinese as *Lee Xiǎo Lóng* (李小龙, Lee Little Dragon). When one thinks of a groundhog, otherwise known as a woodchuck, does the word "strength" come to mind? I guess strength would depend on how much wood a woodchuck could chuck, right? That is, if a wood-chuck could chuck wood. As for wisdom, that's a tough one, too. Is "wisdom" the first thing that comes to mind when you see a woodchuck? Adding insult to injured pride, the Chinese word for "groundhog" is *tǔ bō shǔ* (土拨鼠), which literally translates into "earth dig mouse". Mouse? Really? Is that the best they could do? A groundhog does dig earth, but would be a well-fed mouse. The groundhog is not native to China, but if it was, it would prob-ably be found only on the dinner table. As for luck, the presence of these critters usually symbolizes bad luck and a nasty rodent problem in the works.

So, where does Jesus fit into all this? By chance, pure coin-cidence of course, Candlemas Day also falls on or around the fortieth day after Christmas — or around February 2 — when, according to Luke 2:22–40, Mary and Joseph took their newborn son to the main temple in Jerusalem to perform the redemption of the firstborn as was required by the Law of Moses. It could be

---

47   http://hedgehogcentral.com/hedgehogday.shtml

said that on Candlemas Day, Jesus was making himself known —
a coming out, if you will — just like Puxatawney Phil does every
year in Pennsylvania when he ventures out of his hole to poke
his little head outside to see what's going on; and just like the
Chinese dragon that raises his head to make sure the insects are
behaving and the rains are falling. To clarify for those non-Jews
out there, the redemption of the first born wasn't when Jesus's
little groundhog raised its head to get its good luck haircut. That's
a different ceremony and a different story altogether.

Dragons, Jesus, and Groundhogs. Who would ever think that
these three would have anything at all in common? Better yet,
who thought that February 2 — lunar or solar — was just another
boring winter day?

CHAPTER 13

A LITTLE LESSON ON LOOGIES

SOME CITIES AND COUNTRIES ARE KNOWN FOR WHAT THEIR CITIZENS leave on the ground. For example, the Parisians are infamous for what was once calculated as the 15 metric tons of dog shit[48] they don't bother to clean up each day; and the Taiwanese are known for the brown-red betel nut[49] juice they spit almost everywhere. While the Cambodians are known for their landmines;[50] and the Floridians their alligators,[51] I will always remember China as the loogie capital of the world. For those who are not familiar with the term "loogie" there are other terms which may ring a bell: snot, mucus, booker, spit, boogers, boogies, lung butter, greenie, saliva, and snot rocket. Some of you might only know it by its proper medical term: phlegm. Some of you may just want to stop reading here and skip to the next chapter. Don't say you weren't warned.

Phlegm is the sometimes-chewy material that's carried up into the throat by the wave-like movement of the hairs on the cells lining the trachea and bronchi. Once in the throat, the phlegm is

---

48   http://www.guardian.co.uk/world/2002/apr/12/worlddispatch.jonhenley
49   http://www.angelfire.com/mt/mondotaiwan/culture.html
50   http://www.mekong.net/cambodia/mines.htm
51   http://query.nytimes.com/gst/fullpage.html?res=9D0CE5D6113DF93AA3575
     3C1A967958260 &sec=&spon=&pagewanted=alla

either coughed out, or swallowed after a simple and subtle throat-clearing. The subtle and simple throat clearing has gained with its translation into Chinese, and is pronounced with a loud fingernail-on-chalkboard, throat scraping "hhhhhhhooooooooocccccccccck-kkkkk!" followed by a short pause, then a very audible, aspirated rocket launch to destinations unknown. I'm not sure which one of the four tones of the Chinese language applies, but my guess would be the second (rising) tone.

I didn't really understand the sheer volume of loogies spat out by the Chinese until my trip to Hā'ěrbīn. What suddenly brought the loogie awareness out of my self-imposed denial was that in Hā'ěrbīn, instead of being rubbed into the sidewalk by pedestrians, the loogies froze solid upon contact with the sidewalk and slowly – ever so slowly – evaporated into the bone-dry Siberian air. With so many loogies frozen in time, it became easy to realize how prevalent loogie hocking was among men and women alike. A day in China didn't go by without dodging a loogie.

Loogie hocking knows no boundaries, indoors or out. Sometimes the launcher missed their intended target and they landed on the top rather than in the urinal; at the gym I frequented in Dàlián, I spotted dried loogie stains on the treadmill tread over and over again; and on occasion, I spotted them in elevators.[52] One friend who attended a theatrical performance in Dàlián told me that the guy next to him was hocking so loudly that he was disturbing the performance. While waiting in the Yìwū train station for my train back to Shànghǎi, the guy sitting a few feet across from me quietly dripped a stringy goober from his lips onto the tile floor of the waiting area, and then spread it around with his foot to make it less noticeable and apparently more acceptable. But some people, like the guy walking in front of me during one transfer through the Guǎngzhōu International Airport, didn't let carpeting hold him back, as he shot a slimer onto the floor while he headed to his gate. Using some sort of strange loogie logic, hocking clams willy-nilly in airport terminals and train stations could, to some, be considered marginally acceptable because they are high traffic public places that are, by default, unclean. But one would expect that even the most savage beast would draw the line somewhere, such as in a crowded restaurant. During one dinner in Dàlián, I realized that was only wishful thinking when a Chinese guy, sitting behind and less than one foot away from my coworker's wife, was shooting for a sound effects world championship after he scraped up some goobers from deep-down close to his lungs, and then spat them onto the floor space between his chair and that of my coworker's wife. I guess this is still better than hearing repeated loogie hocking sounds coming from the kitchen in a restaurant while waiting for my food to be served.

---

52 In the elevator of an upper-class Shanghai apartment building in December 2006, I saw a notice in English and Chinese reminding riders that, "Dogs are not allowed to shit in the elevator." At this point, who really cares about loogies?

During one flight into Dàlián I saw and heard one passenger hock up a nice juicy clam and then spit it into a barf bag while we were taxiing to the gate. I gave this guy some credit because the barf bag is a start and signified progress since it was a much better destination than the floor of the plane. But the passenger then neatly folded the bag into its original condition and put it back into the seat back pocket. This wasn't the first time I saw this happen, which means that some percentage of the apparently unused barf bags on any given Chinese airplane have a loogie in it. Maybe that's the reason some Chinese airlines now distribute bags with tear-strips to open the bag, indicating that it's been used. Still, it's best to be careful if anyone ever thinks about making an ad hoc hand puppet to entertain a cranky child.

I wouldn't be a proper engineer without introducing some mathematical or scientific term as it pertains to the ubiquity of Chinese loogies, so I'm going to create a unit of measure: the loogie per square meter, from hereinafter abbreviated as LSM, which will be used to describe the loogie flux of a given piece of surface area. As I have not gone out to actually measure the LSM of a given piece of sidewalk, I'm going to speak in relative terms based on my many hours of walking in Chinese cities. Long stretches of sidewalk tend to have a pretty consistent LSM. This is neither too high nor too low (is there such a thing as "too low"?), but pretty constant as people tend to stay in motion. The LSM starts to increase as one reaches a corner. Loogie launching is as contagious as yawning or scratching an itch: yawn, and someone yawns with you (who yawned just by reading about yawning?); scratch and others will scratch with you (who's feeling itchy?); expel some lung candy and others will expel with you. So, one could say that street corners, where people tend to linger, have a high Loogie Initiation Potential (LIP). When standing at a corner, what is there to do besides look around? Part of looking around is looking down. If someone sees a loogie, I tend to think that the sight of a clam flips an unconscious switch that initiates the whole juicy process.

My master's degree thesis involved the study of crystal growth and crystal growth in space. One of the first things I learned about crystal growth, which is a fancy way of saying "freezing a liquid into a solid", was that for the solid to form, a "seed" was required to start the crystal growing process. Once the seed has formed, it's only a matter of time before the rest of the atoms in the liquid, as the liquid is cooled, line up with the crystal lattice of the seed to form a solid and to grow the crystal. Think rock candy and how it forms when hot water full of dissolved sugar starts to cool down. In loogie-ology, the first loogie on a clean surface could be called Loogie Seed Point (LSP) that increases the LIP to something above zero. Once the LIP becomes greater than zero for that patch of sidewalk, the launcher has created a LSP that will eventually attract loogies from others. LSM (and subsequently LIP) also tend to increase in locations where people tend to linger, such as bus stops and intersections. Another common place where the LSM goes through the roof even though people are in motion, is at the main exit of a building, which in many ways is a good thing.

Once a loogie is created, we all hope that it will eventually be destroyed. To measure that "eventually" there is the Loogie Half-Life (LHL): the time it takes of half of the loogie to disappear from its resting place. Plutonium-239 (Pu-239), which is used in nuclear weapons, has a half-life of 24,100 years. On most days, the loogie half-life seems much, much longer. The LHL never seems to be a short period of time, and unlike Plutonium-239 and other radioactive elements that have a constant half-life no matter where they're located, the LHL can vary with environmental conditions. For example, as demonstrated in Hā'ĕrbīn, the LHL is inversely proportional to the temperature. Colder weather = longer LHL, Warmer = shorter LHL. Also, as seen in Hā'ĕrbīn, once a loogie freezes (does anyone know the heat of fusion of a loogie?), it is less likely to get smeared about from foot traffic. Therefore, at temperatures below freezing the LHL is dependent on its coefficient of diffusion and the moisture concentration gradient between said loogie and the ambient air. The larger the moisture concentration gradient (drier the air), the faster the loogie will sublimate from a solid into a vapor (think dry ice without the smoke). As for any solids – the stuff that makes for a chewy loogie – that may remain, the LHL then becomes dependent on erosion and dilution, as it tends to be in Shànghǎi. It's warmer and rains quite often in Shànghǎi, and there are more people to rub them into the sidewalk. But when there are more people, the LIP, and consequently the LSM increase, which means it's possible for the LSM to reach equilibrium. One could also argue that the LHL is shorter for those loogies located outdoors vs. indoors but that depends on a wide range of variables including the effectiveness and ambition of the housekeeping staff.

I'm sure there's a PhD thesis on human behavior somewhere in this analysis since gooberology could help the Chinese government with their enforcement of their otherwise futile loogie laws. Since the SARS outbreak in March 2003, several unsuccessful public service campaigns and government regulations were put into place to limit those loogie launches. Prior to the 2008 Olympic Games in Běijīng, the government increased its crackdown on spitting, and according to www.china.org.cn, "In Běijīng and Guǎngzhōu, capital of Guǎngdōng[广东] Province, public spitters will have to clean up the phlegm marks and pay a fine of 50 yuan ($6.02). The fine goes up to 200 yuan ($24.10) in Shànghǎi...Guǎngzhōu has also set up cameras in the streets to catch public spitting.[53]" According to the May 5, 2007, *China Daily,* "Běijīng has fined more than 50 people for spitting in the past week's holiday, a report said on Monday, as Běijīng steps up a campaign to 'civilize' the city before the 2008 Olympics.[54]" This was a good start, although it was just 0.00042 percent of the city's total population, and netted the city coffers only $300. If the Běijīng police used the LHL to their advantage to identify where

---

53   http:// www.china.org.cn/english/China/64853.htm
54   http:// www.chinadaily.com.cn/china/2007-05/08/content_867366.htm

the LSM is the highest and where potential LSPs exist, then they could better enforce the loogie law to improve public health as well as generate additional income for the city. But sometimes enforcement can be difficult or nearly impossible if those doing the enforcing don't recognize that there is a problem with the behavior the law is trying to change.

To truly understand the seriousness of this problem, one only needs to consider how many liters of loogie the Chinese let loose annually. With 1.34 billion people in China and assuming that each healthy person expels an estimated 15 to 50 ml/day (0.015 to 0.05 liters per day) of phlegm,[55] and that a conservative 25 percent of the population launches loogies, this means that 5 million gallons of loogie – some of it containing communicable disease – hit the ground in China every day. That's 1.8 billion gallons of lung butter per year, or 3,490 gallons per minute. Yummy. Of course, that's if the population is healthy and only one-fourth of the populations lets their loogies loose. If loogies had the same energy content as gasoline, this would be enough loogie to fuel a 30 mile per gallon car for ten round trips to Pluto each year, assuming that Pluto, at its closest distance to Earth, is 2.67 billion miles away. Solar power, schmolar power. Who needs wind turbines? Loogies are the next big thing in renewable energy.

One important role of an engineer is to perform root cause analysis. If one only solves a symptom – for example, weight loss associated with cancer – without treating the root cause, the problem will only get worse. So goes it with the loogies. The only way to stop loogie launching is to stop them from forming. In my three and a half years living and working in China, I noticed that I was more congested more often, and had more sinus infections during that time than I had in the previous ten. I'm sure it's because of the air pollution and the second-hand cigarette smoke. The Chinese smoke one-third of the world's annual cigarette production. China

55   http://www.answers.com/topic/phlegm

has approximately 350 million smokers, including 70 percent of all Chinese men; and about one million people die each year from smoking-related illness.[56] My non-smoking friends and I, when living in China, said that we had a five-pack-a-day habit although we never picked up a cigarette. I'm also starting to agree with an acquaintance who, over dinner one evening, tried to convince me that nose hairs grow faster in China because the body adapts to the increased air pollution. Chinese air pollution is very serious: my high school friend Jason, who was diagnosed with cystic fibrosis in the 1980s, died in the company of his wife and children in Texas soon after a business trip to China because the air pollution exacerbated his condition. So, if the Chinese government is serious about limiting loogie launching, and the spread of SARS, TB and other communicable diseases, then it might make sense to modify the behaviors of the industrial polluters than the general population. Then again, maybe they're considering another alternative fuel source. Now, it's just a matter of finding a use for all those fast-growing nose hairs...

56   http://www.quitguide.com/smoking-facts.html

CHAPTER 14

HANGING OUT IN HĂINÁN

BY APRIL 2008, A YEAR AND A HALF INTO MY CHINESE ASSIGNMENT, I realized I wasn't seeing as much of China as I first intended. I spent most of the best travel time in 2007 hosting friends and family in Shànghǎi and getting settled in Dàlián. With all that out of the way, it was time to do some exploring on my own to those lesser-known places that first-time visitors to China don't consider. Given that Dàlián was still cold and my hope for an early spring didn't materialize despite the warming signs in Běijīng two months prior, it only made sense to go south.

Usually, when something "goes south" (or, if you're Irish, "goes west"), it means it has changed for the worst. But that's not the case when talking about Sānyà (三亚), on Hǎinán (海南) Island, China. Hǎinán literally translates into Sea (Hǎi) South (Nán), and just happens to be located in the South China Sea. If that wasn't south enough, Sānyà is on the southern shore of Hǎinán Island, making it the southernmost point someone can visit in China, depending on who you talk with and whose maps you're viewing. Hǎinán Island made the international news in 2001 when things really went south after a U.S. Navy EP-3E electronic reconnaissance spy plane made an emergency landing there on April 1 after colliding with a Chinese fighter jet. I didn't travel to Hǎinán to commemorate the seventh anniversary of the spy plane incident, but to relax in the 86-degree weather, soak up some rays, and to do some recon of my own of this famed resort island.

I've never been a big fan of resort hotels since they tend to be nothing more than land-based cruise ships where vacationers are held captive and forced to eat bad food and pay through the nose for a drink. I had done that duty a couple times and knew what to expect. What I did not expect was that I was going to pay 485 RMB ($68.00 at the time) for eight ounces of suntan lotion at the hotel convenience store. Who said capitalism wasn't alive and well in China? I would have carried some with me but didn't really give it any thought. It wouldn't have mattered anyhow, since Chinese airline security adopted the American policies banning liquids and gels in carry-on luggage, and the trip was too short to check a bag.

If I did check a bag, that would have given me a reason to hang out in the baggage claim area of the Sānyà Airport to check out the large crowd of pretty Chinese girls who were waiting for their luggage. But no go. As I passed by the baggage claim area and headed toward the waiting taxis, I realized that the crowd of cuties only confirmed what I had expected when I noticed quite a large number of pretty Chinese girls on my flight from Shànghǎi. Two data points, after all, could very well equal a straight line. Sānyà was going to be a magical place with bikini-clad Chinese nymphets frolicking on the beaches and in the pools. What more could a white guy named *Wěi Tū Lóng* ask for?

Sānyà, on whole, didn't feel like China. The air was fresh, the sky was blue, the smokers were far and few between, and the manicured hotel grounds could have doubled as putting greens. There were no car horns and no loud cell phone talker guys. It was just a laid-back tropical destination. After having spent all my time in China on the mainland, the most striking part about this part of China was the peace and quiet. On my first night in Sānyà, I sat on the balcony of the hotel lobby bar overlooking the pool and the inky darkness beyond it. I knew there were people in Sānyà, since our Boeing 737 was full and the flight I originally wanted to take was also completely full, but there was no telling so from that night on the balcony.

Located at the same latitude as the northern Philippines, and only a stone's throw from Thailand, Laos, and Cambodia, the culture of Sānyà seemed as disconnected from China as Hăinán Island is from the Chinese mainland. The only Chinese people I encountered were those who worked at the hotel, and many of them were not Han Chinese, but looked as if they were from the neighboring countries. Mixing things up a bit, the food and drink menus were in English and Russian. At one point I even forgot that I was in China. With the Chinese population, oddly, in short supply, I found myself mostly in the company of Canadians, Brits, Americans, and Russians. Especially the Russians. After my first day, I realized that my hotel was a big Russian hangout. And let me tell you: did they hang out. If I ever had to open a strength testing facility for high performance swimwear fabrics, then the Holiday Inn Resort on Sānyà Bay would be where I'd set up shop. Most of the spandex-clad Russian women were past the point of no return to Babushkadom, including the pregnant or overweight women in the thong bikinis, and really, I don't want to ruin your next meal by describing the men. If the Russian women in Sānyà looked like the Russian hotties in Dàlián then I wouldn't be complaining, but there comes a time when people need to realize that common decency and their perceived sense of style may not necessarily align. The multitude of scantily-clad Chinese nymphets I was expecting was nowhere to be found at the hotel or on the beach. The two or three I saw all weekend were hanging off the arms of doughy, pear-shaped, middle-aged (i.e., wealthy) Chinese men who, like the Russians, should have covered up or stayed in their rooms.

I was surprised at how few people were on the beach given the number of hotels located along the seaside. I took a stroll one day and came across a couple people fishing, a Chinese couple having their wedding photos taken, a few others also out for a stroll, a couple in the water, and a Russian woman sunning herself while reading a book. Otherwise, the beach was mine. The beach at Sānyà Bay was empty. Empty of people, that is. The beach could have used a good combing since the people in Sānyà City – visible from my hotel on Sānyà Bay – subscribed to the "big ocean, big toilet" philosophy when it came to disposing their household garbage. There were the remnants of instant noodle containers; glass vials what once contained the bitter concoctions of traditional Chinese medicine that help the locals hang on; loads of Styrofoam, dead fish, orange peels, coconut shells, random pieces of plastic, and hundreds of cigarette butts. Even if Sānyà Bay wasn't full of litter, I seriously doubted that I would swim there. Besides the garbage, I saw the carcass of a 16-inch diameter jellyfish. When I described the jellyfish to one British couple who escaped from the northern industrial city of Tiānjīn (天津), they told me they saw plenty more similarly-sized jellyfish a couple days earlier. Going from the top of the food chain to the bottom was as easy as stepping into the sea...

...or partaking in the "Hot Spring Fish Massage Therapy" offered by my hotel. It's not someone taking a smelly cooked fish and rubbing it into one's skin. Rather, it was a massage in a pool of warm water full of live fish. When someone stepped into the pool, hundreds of hungry minnows flocked over to the person to exfoliate them by eating their dead layer of exposed skin. The massage part happened when the fish used their mouths to "bite" off the skin. The fish don't have teeth that break the skin, but only rough gums. Picture a toothless granny trying to eat corn on the cob. Still, it was a bit creepy as hundreds of fish swam over to eat my feet. Some people sat neck deep in the pool, but I was wearing a pair of relatively loose fitting swim shorts and I wasn't interested in having fish biting in places that were not meant to be bitten.

As I sat there with my feet in the pool and the fish nibbling away, I started to realize that I should have known better than to expect to find those Chinese nymphets exposing themselves to the sun. While the white people (self included) spent entire days lounging under the hot midday sun alongside the giant two-level pool complete with waterfalls, a few Chinese people would venture out to find a shady spot. It was only after the shadows of the palm trees started to grow long that the Chinese considered venturing outdoors. Unlike Western cultures where tanned skin is a sign of wealth and considered a positive trait (tanned vacationers have the time and money to take a vacation; the cliché dream of some Western women is to meet someone who is "tall, dark and handsome") this is not the case in China. Tanned people, to the Chinese and most Asian cultures, are considered farmers, street urchins, laborers, and of a lower, poorer class of people who work outdoors for a living, i.e., rednecks. To be fashionable and beautiful, the Chinese strive for pale skin. It was contradictory – almost wrong – for the Chinese to flock to their very own tropical paradise with sea, surf, and sun, but not take full advantage of the first two because of the third. I wasn't complaining because this worked to the advantage of the Westerners who need not worry about fighting the Chinese for the lounge chairs. I guess I need to do some more asking around to better understand why the Chinese would go to Sānyà but never go outdoors. In a culture of savers, it would have been cheaper for the Chinese to stay home.

In Sānyà I felt as though I had left China behind, but was occasionally reminded that it wasn't too far away. On the way from the airport to my hotel, my taxi passed by a couple of out-door karaoke machines at roadside food stalls where Chinese men were trying to croon at 200 decibels to an audience of empty tables and chairs. My hotel was catering a conference of Chinese computer scientists and engineers (no nymphets in that crowd), who, when they walked past the pool, brought with them a cloud of cigarette smoke reminiscent of Pigpen's dust cloud; and I only heard one loogie hocker all weekend, a Chinese woman walking on the beach about twenty feet behind me. Unfortunately, Karen Carpenter already made inroads to this otherwise non-Chinese part of China; and I saw a Chinese guy request that the hotel's Filipino band play the *Titanic* theme song by Celine Dion, which made me fully understand why Chinese guys don't float the boats of white women. When it was time to leave for the airport to head back to Dàlián, I realized China was only five feet from the front door of my hotel the whole time because I had to negotiate a fair fare with my cabbie who then tried to sell me hookers – gesturing with both hands just in case I didn't understand his English – for the entire 15-minute trip.

In all, it was a good two days of lazing under the sun. It was just what I needed to recharge, and it allowed me to see another, very different part of China. It's just too bad I didn't go where I thought I was going. When I returned to Dàlián, my American coworker told me that she and her husband had just returned from Sānyà and raved about their week on the beach at Yàlóng Bay (亚龙湾). When I made my plans, I found a hotel rate about half the cost of what she paid but didn't pay attention to the location. In the big scheme of things, it wasn't a big deal because I now have an excuse to make a return trip to Sānyà if I ever find myself facing down another Manchurian winter.

CHAPTER 15

RUNNING: DÀLIÁN-STYLE

OVER THE YEARS I'VE FOUND THAT THERE IS NO BETTER, LIVER-FRIENDLY way to cleanse the brain after a shitty day at the office than a good run. When I first volunteered for a long-term expat assignment in China, I knew that one of the sacrifices I would have to make was distance running in the form of marathons and half-marathons. Dàlián, with its 5-million-plus people and resultant traffic and air pollution, was not necessarily compatible with outdoor running. It was a big switch from Portland, Oregon, where clean and green running trails go on for miles. And honestly, there were just too many other distractions in the form of travel and sightseeing to remain disciplined about the whole running thing. Long gone were the days when half-marathons were just mere weekend training runs. The extent of my outdoor running in Dàlián consisted of a handful of car-dodging adventures on the perimeter road of Xīnghǎi Square; or my inconsistent attempts to develop an early Saturday morning routine along Dàlián's Golden Pebble Beach (Jīnshíitān, 金石滩) with a few friends. The balance of my running was limited to three-mile jaunts on the treadmill at my local gym just because the boredom wouldn't let me run any farther. Still, I couldn't pass up the chance to run my first official half-marathon in almost three years at the 23ʳᵈ China Sports Lottery Cup Dàlián International Marathon held on April 26, 2009.

When I went to collect my race number the day before the race, I thought the race organizers made a mistake. My number was 24. I usually get three- and four-, and sometimes five-digit numbers typical of the average plodder, not two-digit numbers which are generally reserved for elite runners. Sometimes the Chinese get confused about foreigners (some Chinese friends privately admitted that there are times when all white people look alike), but I'm almost positive it's difficult to confuse me with a Kenyan. Then again, maybe because I was a foreigner people thought I traveled to Dàlián just for the running experience (and the $25,000 first prize plus $5,000 bonus if the winner completed the race under two hours and fifteen minutes) like the elites did. The only problem was that there is nothing elite about my running except for its mediocrity.

I was a bit surprised to learn that Dàlián even had an annual marathon and half-marathon, or could even attract enough attendees since the Chinese, beyond their amazing Olympic performance in 2008, didn't seem to be the most athletic of people. Sleepers are more common than runners. Chinese people can sleep anywhere, anytime, at the drop of a hat. The only Chinese I saw doing any serious running were a team of Olympic hopefuls in training that I sometimes passed on my pre-dawn commutes to work; those who overslept and were trying to catch the bus that was pulling away; or those who tried their luck crossing several lanes of speeding traffic. Expending energy on miscellaneous recreational endeavors is a luxury characteristic of a well-developed middle class with a well-developed middle section and plenty of surplus energy to burn. I can safely say that I never saw an overweight Chinese farmer or manual laborer.

With the seemingly large number of running novices, it made perfect sense for the race organizers to provide, along with the race number and the color-coded race t-shirt, a pamphlet with race logistics, rules, and advice to ensure everyone had a safe and healthy run. For example:

- *"The players of the Mini-marathon item have no limits to age and sex.*

- *"Players with the following diseases should not participate in the race: Congenital heart disease and rheumatic heart disease; Hypertension and cerebral vascular diseases; Myocarditis and other heart disease; Coronary artery disease and severe arrhythmia; Diabetes mellitus with too high or too little glucose; Others that is not fit for sports.*

- *"Athletes without [timing] chip will have no achievement.*

- *"Running Marathon is a mind and physical challenges, but we should put safety for the first goal, and therefore we have to learn 'giving up.'*

- *"Exercise properly for 30 minutes before the race: one is to improve their own body temperature and the other is to prevent heart movement.*

- *"Athletes who are obesity and have thicker tendon have to rub Vaseline ointment at the crotch to prevent skin injury.*

- *"Because some people have unmentionable diseases (some diseases have not been found by their own yet.), if they take part in the race with larger tension and intensity, their unmentionable diseases will possibly outbreak and have accidents.*

- *"For the normal people who had check-up, if they have one of the following circumstances, they should not take part in the race: heart rate up to 85 times per minute when in silence; blood pressure above 140/90 mmHg; coronary heart disease, frequent arrhythmia, sexual conduction block and other cardiovascular diseases...*

- *"Marathon Sports is a long-distance aerobic exercise, before the race it should stimulate the excitement of the central nervous system so that various systems of the body (muscles, blood system, respiratory system, exercise system) can establish coordination, and all this can be achieved by gradual warming up."*

Since I hadn't run distance in a while, I took their advice and showed up to the starting line about an hour early to do some stretching in the crisp morning air. While stretching, I saw that the participants for the 5K charity run were sorting themselves out. As part of the charity run, employees of foreign companies in Dàlián raised money and volunteered to escort handicapped runners. Not far from me was group of people wearing white bibs with big red print that said "Blind" in English and Chinese. A few seconds later I saw a group wearing bibs that said, "Deaf". I couldn't help but wonder where the dumb people were hanging out, but the smell of cigarette smoke wafting through the air told me they were not too far away.

By chance, the starting and finishing lines were two blocks from my apartment, so there was no need for me to pack a gear bag. I had with me only the necessities: shorts, shirt, shell, shoes, socks, shades, and Shuffle (iPod, that is). While walking around the starting area, the Chinese crowds kept staring at me. The sun was not yet high enough for shades, but I donned mine so I could get a better look at the crowd. By race day I had been in China long enough to phase out all the staring people, but on this particular day there were more than usual. When I entered a crowd, I parted it like Moses did the Red Sea. They all gave me space, which was not a typical behavior in China. On a couple of occasions, groups that were noisily chatting would stop, stare at me as I walked by, and then whispered among themselves while looking in my direction. Several times while stretching, some Chinese runners asked if they could have their photo taken with me. My number was covered under my warm-up shell, and my eyes with shades, but I guess they thought that I was in good shape and had the look of some sort of elite runner. Some were polite to ask for photos, but others snuck a shot or two from a respectable distance. If they only knew they were wasting their time and film or memory on an average John.

Now, not only did I have a number I had to live up to, but the Chinese, with their attention, put some pretty high expectations on my performance. The pressure was on and stage fright was setting in. Little did they know that my only goal was to finish before the sweeper van pulled me off the course. Hedging my bets, I ran with the South African doctor who was part of my Saturday morning group. As the time ticked down to the start of the race, I started thinking through all the standard stuff: Did I get all my stretching in? Did I need to use the toilet? I ate properly that morning, but what do I do when I start getting hungry (no sports gels in China)? Was I properly hydrated? At what pace should I start? What was I forgetting? ...and the list went on. But the more I thought about all these things, I began to default to the tried-and-true method of finishing a long distance race: pace a few feet behind the cutest girl, and hopefully pick one that didn't have a boyfriend/husband/girlfriend, thick tendons, sexual conduction block, or any unmentionable diseases. It wasn't until halfway through the race when I realized that this was a flawed strategy: skinny Chinese girls didn't have a lot of miscellaneous energy to expend on distance running, which defies some sort of law of physics given the sheer amount of food a skinny Chinese girl can consume in one sitting.

Dàlián put on its Sunday best that morning: clear blue skies, bright sunshine, city streets devoid of cars and buses but lined with the police hotties. The marathon was a two-lap, east-west, dual out-and-back (visualize a figure eight) that consisted of

long gradual hills and a few flat spots. The last three miles of
the New York City Marathon came to mind, but over and over
again. The Siberian winds that never stop blowing helped in spots
by pushing us up a couple of the hills, but the occasional gusts
pushed everyone around the course. Crowds of the young and
old, dragon dancers, drum beaters, and high school bands, all
cheered *jiā yóu!* (加油!), which literally translates into "refuel!"
and loosely translates into "come on!", for the Chinese, and *lǎo
wài jiā yóu!* (老外加油!) for me – the *lǎo wài* or "old foreigner"
– and the couple dozen other foreigners among the 10,000-strong
field. The only white spectator I saw for 13.1 miles gave me an
enthusiastic high-five as if I was representing the entire race for
him. The Dàlián I saw that morning was the way Dàlián should
be. If only Dàlián could be that way every day, or at least once
a week. The Mayor of Dàlián should consider starting a Sunday
Street Closure like in Bogota, Paris, San Francisco, and Tokyo,
and giving the streets to runners, walkers, cyclists, kite flyers, and
rollerbladers. There was something to be said for running down
the middle of Dàlián's main thoroughfare, Zhōngshān Road, past
City Hall and People's Square, and jamming out to Springsteen's
"Born in the U.S.A." I still visualize that singular moment – blue
sky, cool morning air, yellow sunshine, and the people lining the
street – every time I hear the song.

Leg cramps at the 10-mile point started to ruin my day. Xīnghǎi
Square was closed to traffic and I missed the taxi drivers I usually
saw at Xīnghǎi because dodging them gave me something to think
about besides running. Still, the cramps were nothing that Nick-
elback, Prince and the Revolution, Daughtry, Fergie, Kiss, OAR,
Guns 'n Roses, U2, Whitesnake, Don McLean, Matchbox Twenty,
and a couple stretch breaks couldn't cure. As I headed into the last
long hill, I had to stop again to stretch my protesting calves that
hadn't seen that type of exercise in a very long time. It was just then
that iPod Shuffle fate took over and The Boss returned to carry me
across the finish line in 2 hours and 4 minutes with "Born to Run".

It wasn't my best time, and it wasn't my worst, so all in all it was an average race on a kick-ass Spring day in Dàlián. Eleven minutes and ten expensive seconds later, the first elite runner crossed the finish line. I briefly took some comfort knowing that I beat the first elite finisher across the finish line, but I ran one lap to his two. Oh well, you can't win them all. Just don't tell all the Chinese who put my picture into their photo albums!

CHAPTER 16

GOING BLAND IN Běijīng

WHEN I RETURNED TO PORTLAND, OREGON IN JUNE 2008 TO ATTEND A friend's wedding, many people kept asking me about the 2008 Běijīng Olympics and, since I lived a short flight away from Běijīng, whether or not I was planning on attending. I gave them a quick and definite "No way!" When they gave me a puzzled look, I told them Běijīng was a place worth avoiding in August. It's hot, it's humid, it's crowded, and it's polluted. It would be like the equivalent of holding the Olympic Games in Houston, Texas in August, but with more people, more pollution, and all the hotels and restaurants taking advantage of the Olympic hype. Making an Olympic trip to Beijing even worse would be all the foreign tourists and all the Chinese looking to separate said tourists from their money. That was the easy explanation. It was the other explanation that was a bit harder to convey.

As it happened, prior to my flight to Portland that June, I spent a hot and humid evening in Běijīng, which further reinforced my decision to not return in August. You see, each time I return to Běijīng I can't help but think about my first trip there in October 2004. Back then, all I had with me was a bag of clothes, phrase book, tour book, map, some general thoughts of what I wanted to do, and a sense of adventure. I accept that firsts can't

be surpassed, as numerous subsequent trips to Běijīng have demonstrated, but I still walk some of the same streets, and compare
the city to that first trip. I am still quite fond of my first days of
exploring what I considered a crazy, exotic city, which may be
the reason why on that particular June evening the changes that
occurred since October 2004 – I'm sure mostly because of the
Olympics – seemed all that more poignant.

As the old English Proverb goes, "all good things must come
to an end." One could argue that on August 8, 2008, at 8:08 p.m.,[57]
at the start of the opening ceremonies for the Běijīng Olympics,
Old Běijīng officially came to an end. But the end had already
started years prior when 1.5 million Chinese residents were relo-
cated to make way for the Olympic venues.[58] In other parts of
Běijīng where Olympic venues were not built, I witnessed the
city's gradual facelift. Hutongs – the traditional Běijīng neigh-
borhoods where I spent hours exploring the narrow alleys, and
watching life as it had been lived for over a hundred years – were
being, and continue to be replaced by sterile high-rise apartments
or glass-covered office buildings. To make matters even worse, the
demise of Chinglish is right around the corner. The Běijīng City
Government attempted to remove Chinglish from all city signs
before the start of the Olympic Games, even calling upon Western
expats in the city to volunteer for the effort.[59] When I first visited
Běijīng, I bumped into a few foreigners here and there, and there
was an instant bond of camaraderie because even in this national
capital full of foreign embassies, we were a rare breed. Today there
are so many foreigners in Běijīng that I rarely look up to give
a passing glance. If you want a unique experience, go find The
Tree in the Sānlǐtún (三里屯) Bar District, which is just around the
corner from Poacher's Bar. They serve the best wood-fired pizza
in Běijīng, complimented with a full selection of German and Bel-

---

57   The number "8" in China symbolizes wealth and prosperity.
58   http://www.usatoday.com/sports/olympics/2007-06-05-3431055449_x.htm
59   http://en.epochtimes.com/news/7-2-20/51962.html

gian beers. When inside, take a look around. You will think you walked right out of China and straight into San Francisco.

In 2004 Běijīng, being a six-foot-four-inch white guy came with a something akin to, for the lack of a better term, rock-star status. That meant I attracted all sorts of unwanted attention. After a week in Shànghǎi in September 2003, where I couldn't swing a cat without hitting a hooker, I had expectations of what I would encounter while flying solo in Běijīng and Xī'ān (西安) in 2004. But I was approached by only one Chinese hooker during that two-week trip. In the matter of a year I went from being a rock star to being a wash out. What kind of white guy can't attract a Chinese hooker? This left me thinking for months about some fatal flaw I must have possessed that, if it repelled the most hardened of Chinese hookers, would make any normal good girl run for the hills. It was not until I returned to Shànghǎi in March 2005 when I realized that the hooker phenomena I experienced had nothing to do with my mojo (to my relief, I had been out of my Shànghǎi hotel for five minutes before being propositioned), but everything to do with the differences between the more traditional and conservative Běijīng and the more progressive and capitalistic Shànghǎi. But by June 2008, Běijīng was closing in on Shànghǎi because there were more hookers on the streets. I passed by one group of about ten girls – all very cute, very friendly, wanting to know where I was from, where I was going, blah, blah, blah – prowling in the Guómào (国贸) area of the Chāoyáng District (朝阳区) popular with foreigners and diplomats, each looking to participate in some international athletic events of their own.

As more foreign companies opened up shop or expanded their existing operations in China, a flood of foreigners rode into town on the expat gravy train with their bags of cash, helping the city's residents climb their way up the social ladder. These days, the Běijīng residents seem much more affluent and a much more cosmopolitan compared to their comrades living in Tier 2 and Tier 3 cities. Earning more than just a subsistence wage, the Běijīngers now have more discretionary income for stashing away; buying their first apartment or possibly their second or third which will generate rental income; and for shopping, albeit not yet enough to transition China's export economy into a consumer-led one. Still, Běijīngers in 2010 bought 800,000 cars, and the number of cars on the Beijing streets more than quadrupled to 4.76 million between 1997 and 2010, prompting city officials to open a license plate lottery to limit car sales to 240,000 per year.[60] On the plus side, the all-day bumper to bumper traffic is a good way to keep down the number of traffic fatalities. Today, the previously ubiquitous bicycle seems quaint and inadequate.

With all those cars on the road – and all the building construction throughout the city – it didn't take long for me in 2004 to develop a case of congestion, a cough, and a sore throat commonly known as "Běijīng Throat." The 2008 Běijīng Olympics made sure the big particles floating in the air that got caught in throats disappeared, but the invisible particles that lodge deep in lungs are still there. Běijīng is much tidier because an army of sanitation workers is constantly on litter patrol, even in the subways. In this same city where, in 1946, Chairman Mao told the country to dig up their flowers and grass because they were too bourgeois, more and more flowers appear along the highways each year. Běijīngers respect their city, but that same attention to care cannot be found in the out-of-town Chinese visitors.

These days, I don't suffer through Běijīng Throat and the number of blue-sky days in the city increased from 100 in 1998 to 246 in 2010 and then increased again to 274 in 2011,[61, 62] even through the gray days feel like no progress has been made to fix the air. To give Běijīng residents incentive to stop driving and to make it easier to get around, more than 10,000 workers constructed 52 new, crisp, clean subway stations and 54 miles of new

60   http://www.china.org.cn/business/2011-01/27/content_21826885.htm
61   http://www.nytimes.com/2008/01/10/world/asia/10china.html
62   http://www.chinadaily.com.cn/china/2011-12/18/content_14282398.htm

track that brought the total length of the Běijīng subway to 186 miles.[63] In 2004, there were no air conditioned subway cars on the two subway lines, but today they're the norm on all 15 lines. By 2015, Běijīng is expected to have 321 miles of subway, making it the longest subway in the world. For those heading to Běijīng, the best subway line for sightseeing is Line #5 (Purple) connecting the Temple of Heaven and the Lama Temple. When at the Lama Temple make sure to find the Confucius school, and then wander through the remaining Hutongs toward the Bell and Drum Towers.

Not only did Běijīng put on a cleaner, happier face for the Olympics, so did some of the American companies in China that had been operating otherwise for years. Across China not too long ago, almost all the aluminum soda and beer cans had the pull and toss tabs, those pesky tabs that cut feet on beaches, got stuck in throats, etc., that were once commonplace in the U.S. until the early 1980s. When the West moved to the current, safer stay-tab design, the old manufacturing equipment went east. In the few months leading up to the Olympics the multinational firms selling beverages in China moved to the stay-tab design, but some of the older designs can still be found. There are also other positives that the Běijīng Olympics brought to China. For example, the most notable were my Olympic heroes, namely the French security detail in Paris who failed to hold back the Tibetan protesters who tried to grab the Olympic torch from the arms of Jīn Jīng (金晶) the one-legged, wheelchair-bound Chinese paralympian fencer. Because the French flubbed Jīn's security detail, I was able to shop in relative peace and quiet in my local (French-owned) Carrefour supermarket for most of the summer because the Chinese shoppers boycotted it.

As I headed to the Běijīng International Airport that June morning to finish my trip to Portland, I had to face the truth about the changes in Běijīng. Across the street from my hotel was the

---

63 http://www.haww.gov.cn/html/20070514/527260.html

73-storey, 1,083 feet China World Trade Center that was an empty lot in 2004. Of course, on this early morning, I wished that the building was the only reminder of what Běijīng was becoming. I also had to deal with a lazy Běijīng cabbie. There was a time when taxi drivers were friendly and eager to do business with whoever jumped into their cab. But now, the rank of lazy cabbies is growing longer by the day. On previous visits to Běijīng, one cabbie wouldn't take me to a place because it was "too close", and another wouldn't take me somewhere because it was "too far" away. In October 2011, the cabbies just refused to pick me up.

As I walked out of my hotel on that morning in 2008, the cabbie – standing outside his car and about 30 feet from me – asked me in Chinese, "Where you go?"

"You come here," I said in Mandarin.

One he drove over and I was in his car with my luggage, I told him I wanted to go to the airport, and we engaged in some friendly chit-chat about the weather, etc. Even though he had a white guy in his car who demonstrated some knowledge of Mandarin, the cabbie tried to take the long way to the airport.

"Where you go?" I asked, as he was getting ready to head south through an intersection.

"To the airport," the cabbie replied.

"But the way to the airport is back there to the north. You need to turn left and then turn left again."

Realizing that he had been called out, the cabbie stayed quiet for the rest of the trip. Once we made it to the airport, the meter read 67 RMB ($9.71 at the time). The total fare, including the toll, came to 77 RMB.

"You give me 100 RMB," demanded the cabbie. I wouldn't budge from the meter reading, so he grudgingly took the 77 RMB that he earned as I reassured him that he would soon see plenty of foreigners happy to pay him 100 RMB to the airport.

In retrospect, the most discouraging part of my overnight stay in Běijīng was the cabbie's sense of entitlement. This was the most off-putting, since it reminded me of what awaited me at the other end of my journey that day; and what I would once again be faced with on a daily basis after I repatriated to the U.S.

Douglas Adams, the British author of *The Hitchhiker's Guide to the Galaxy*, wrote, "Human beings, who are almost unique in having the ability to learn from the experience of others, are also remarkable for their apparent disinclination to do so.[64]" With each day, Běijīng is looking and feeling a lot more like Shànghǎi, and Shànghǎi has already started to feel a lot more like New York City except with 22 million Chinese people. Let's just hope Běijīng's leaders are a bit more inclined to ensure that their city does not turn into yet another bland, homogenous victim of globalization.

64 Adams, Douglas, *The Hitchhiker's Guide to the Galaxy*, Harmony Books, New York, New York, 1979.

CHAPTER 17

HOOKERS, SPIES, CROOKS...

...AND THE OCCASIONAL BUSINESSMAN, I'M SURE, ARE ALL FREQUENT guests of the Zurich airport hotel in which I stayed at the end of a July 2008 business trip. That's Zurich as in Zurich, Switzerland – not Zurich, Montana, 59547, population 40 – home to billions of dollars in anonymous cash. First of all, there is no greater hooker magnet than a captive nomadic population thousands of miles from home, flush with cash and with empty beds upstairs. Of course, where there's money there are crooks. Because money can buy influence and information, and spies are always looking for leverage for recruiting purposes, they come to the party with their own cash. Movers, shakers, deal makers and deal breakers, I'm sure, have all spent at least one night in this particular hotel.

Over the years I've spent a fair bit of time in countless hotels in dozens of countries. Many are just a blur but once in a while some truly stand out for their location, service, luxury, friendliness, emptiness, cleanliness, overall uniqueness, number of permanent residents on social services, etc. Still, even after some half-dozen stays over just as many years, no hotel intrigues me more than this one. If I had to choose a Zurich hotel on my own, this one wouldn't have been my first pick. Ever since a friend introduced it to me in 2001, I keep it in my back pocket for whenever I have an early morning flight out of Zurich. The hotel has turned into a pleasant, although somewhat spendy, surprise. If I had to come up with a list of the top fifty best people watching places in the world, this hotel and the Zurich International Airport would rank near the top.

A quick stroll through the hotel lobby revealed a turbaned Indian man, others of Middle Eastern descent, a young Turkish man using a pay phone, an American who looked like a banker, and a gaggle of Asian women just back from a shopping spree, loaded down with bags advertising luxury brands. There is plenty – almost an abnormally high – amount of seating for a hotel lobby. Most seats were empty, and those who occupied the seats went out of their way to be as far away as possible from others who were seated. In one corner, two smartly-dressed middle-aged men, side-by-side, were quietly discussing something over a ciga-rette and a bottle of sparkling water. In another corner, there were a couple of serious men who seemed intent on people watching. I think they were the spies, but probably not the only spies.

This hotel is unique because it happens to be located in a country that is at the crossroads of Europe and the Middle East. Like at any crossroads, people come from and go in all sorts of directions. Between 8:55 a.m. and 11:40 a.m. on July 18, 2008, flights were leaving Zurich for Vienna, Riga, Dresden, Brussels, St. Petersburg, Punta Cana, Amsterdam, Prague, Tivat (Monte-negro), Tel Aviv, Cairo, Mumbai, Paris, Toronto, Skopje, Buda-pest, Sarajevo, London, Philadelphia, New York City, Frankfurt, Warsaw, Dusseldorf, Copenhagen, Istanbul, Pristina, Helsinki, Alicante, Belgrade, Moscow, Koeln (Cologne, Germany), and Rome. I'm sure I spent the night in the same hotel as a few of those airline passengers. On the shuttle from the hotel to the air-port, there were two Israelis, a half-dozen Japanese, at least one American, and a Hungarian woman. On the same shuttle a few years prior, the hookers were headed to the hotel.

Maybe I'm too much of a cynic, but I don't believe that the motives of all these people – such as the hookers – were pure. But I guess it all depends on one's definition of "pure". Ok, I'll cut some slack for the family of five and the traveling orchestra made up of high school girls from Western Australia, but in the traveling population as large as that at the Zurich International Airport, statistics and the Bell Curve dictate that some have, are, or will be engaged in questionable activities that they want to keep secret. Maybe it's the elitism that comes to mind when people mention places like St. Moritz and Davos, where the lifestyles of the rich, influential, and famous are out of reach and opaque to us mere middle-class mortals. It could also be that many of the world's crooks, dictators, and oligarchs have stashed away their millions and billions in any number of Swiss banks. An Indian business acquaintance who traveled with me on that 2008 trip to Switzerland recalled his childhood years in India when he heard about government leaders diverting public money to Switzerland. Nothing breeds suspicion more than the lack, or the perception of a lack, of transparency.

The perceived veil of secrecy that hangs over Zurich may be much simpler and much more innocent. Maybe all my cynicism comes from reading too many spy novels like those written by bestselling authors Gayle Lynds and Tom Clancy, or watching too many James Bond movies even though only three Bond films contained scenes from Switzerland. But Switzerland's biggest mystery of all – next to the disposition of all the Jewish and Nazi gold – is how a land-locked country won the America's Cup international sailing championships in 2003 and again in 2007. One can only wonder if any Swiss Navy Personal Lubricants[65] were used to turn that team into a well-oiled machine.

Maybe my cynicism is also based on the fact that spies really do conduct their business in Zurich. Just ask Brian Patrick Regan,

---

65   http://www.swissnavylubes.com

who was convicted on February 20, 2003, in U.S. Federal Court on two counts of attempted espionage. He was apprehended at Dulles International Airport as he was boarding a plane for his second trip to Zurich; or Aldrich Ames, convicted in 1994 and considered to be the spy who did the most damage to the U.S. intelligence services, who opened two bank accounts in Zurich just to do something with all the cash he was piling up from his Russian handlers. And let's not forget American Harold (Jim) Nicholson, convicted of spying in 1997, who met with his Russian SVR handlers in Zurich. I wonder if any of them ever stayed at my hotel...

I envy the Swiss. It's good to be Swiss. The Swiss kick ass, literally, since their army is undefeated. Apparently there is also a well-oiled Navy somewhere, since its existence was validated by some random guy who once tried to sell me a Swiss Navy Knife, Watch, and Pen set at a gas station in a Newark, New Jersey neighborhood. Spend enough time in Switzerland, and you'll hear stories about the fighter jets that supposedly land on runways inside mountain caves, and see the tell-tale manhole covers on the tank traps. Having an Army, Navy and Air Force could be a bit excessive given that Switzerland is a neutral country, but someone needs to defend the borders and protect the Pope.

Neutrality works in their favor because the Swiss become everyone's friends, and the Swiss can travel to every country in the world. I have one Swiss friend who, during the last 30 years, has worked in over 80 countries including Iran, Iraq, Israel, Saudi Arabia, the U.S., Russia, China and Malaysia. In Switzerland, there's no such thing as the Axis of Evil. Citizens of all countries can be found in Switzerland because Switzerland is the home to many United Nations offices. Eventually, vacationers and businessmen from all these countries that don't necessarily have positive relations with each other might just one day happen to stay at my airport hotel where they may have a friendly, casual chat beyond the view of the international media and the wing-nut ideologues back home. The World Economic Forum's week-long meeting held in the mountain village of Davos, Switzerland, each year is a fine example of where this happens regularly. My airport hotel is probably the closest thing to Utopia on the face of the planet today, with all nationalities peacefully tolerating each other under the same roof. I'm sure the hotel bar has something to do with it.

After a week of business meetings from breakfast until after dinner, I could have spent the evening in the hotel bar but opted for a quiet meal and an early night. Instead of taking a 50 SFr ($49 at the time) taxi for the six-mile ride into downtown Zurich, I decided to have dinner in one of the hotel restaurants. There, I found over a hundred hungry souls with apparently the same idea. Around me were families with kids, a table of six with one guy who was dressed just a little too well for eating in that particular hotel restaurant, a handful of retired couples, and a dozen or so stylish women oozing European chic scattered throughout the place. The restaurant management truly understood their customer base: When I asked for a table for one, I was seated at a table barely big enough for one place setting, salt and pepper shakers, a wine glass, and a small vase with a flower. As I sat there with the latest edition of the *Economist*, and what amounted to a $36 dinner consisting of a salad and a glass of wine, I scanned the room once again. But this time I didn't see any diners.

Instead, I saw that my waitress was friends with two of the chic European women, apparently regulars, who sat at the table across from me. I then looked to my right and saw two other women chatting in German over glasses of wine, then two others sitting adjacent to the first pair. The airport hotel restaurant was an awfully expensive place for girlfriends to catch up with each other. I then reminded myself that all the women were not necessarily there for dinner, but instead were looking for some extra special dessert. As I sat at my table for one with my magazine, the sharks were circling the bait. From a previous encounter in this hotel, I already knew how this game played out. Not wanting to call any attention to myself, I kept reading, finished my dinner, paid my bill, and called it a night.

There's something that completely fascinates me with this particular hotel, and I think it has more to do with myself than those I had so much fun observing. As I was checking in, the receptionist handed me a glass of champagne. After she gave me my room keycard, I walked through the lobby and into the elevator. As the elevator moved toward the sixth floor, I pondered my reflection in a mirror. There I was with my bag of clothes over my shoulder, a laptop bag in tow, all the while sipping the glass of champagne. What struck me most was that I had trouble adjudicating that moment with my redneck childhood in Massena. Who was that guy I was looking at and where and how did he come into being? To everyone else, I could have been the hooker, the crook, the spy, or the occasional businessman. Then again, to steal a phrase from the 1985 John Hughes movie *The Breakfast Club*, "maybe those are the simplest terms and most convenient definitions." Maybe each one of us is, in some way, a hooker, a crook, a spy, and an occasional businessman. I was once a consultant so that could technically classify me as a prostitute, crook, and a businessman. But one thing is for sure: When you are at this particular Zurich airport hotel you can pretend to be whomever you want. Just don't forget who you really are and from where you came.

And one last thing: when you're done pretending, don't forget to try their ice cream.

CHAPTER 18

EXPLORING CAMBODIA

WHEN I WAS IN ELEMENTARY SCHOOL, I HEARD ABOUT BAD THINGS HAP-pening in Cambodia mainly because a quiet Cambodian girl named Cindy showed up at our school. I never understood Pol Pot, the Khmer Rouge or what was happening in that part of the world in the 1970s and early 1980s, but now looking back on it all, it had to have been bad if a Cambodian girl was escaping to Massena. Since then, the only things I ever heard about Cambodia involved civil war, genocide, land mines, poverty, pedophilia and famine. Still, I never comprehended or understood Cambodia. Deep in the recesses of my brain, Cambodia had a very high "yuck factor" and never made it onto the list of places I wanted to visit. But after three friends returned from separate trips to Cambodia with rave reviews, I opted to hit the jungle and follow in the footsteps of Lara Croft for the October 2008 Chinese National holiday instead of ruining my liver and skin on the beaches of Thailand or Indonesia.

In Cambodia, where the average income is $200 per month — the United Nations Development Program estimated in 2010 that a third of the population makes less than $1.00 per day — one is constantly reminded of the grinding poverty, but I encountered and sensed very little misery among the everyday people. People

didn't focus on what they didn't have, but were content with what they possessed. I've seen more misery in Portland, Oregon, where the average welfare recipient sees government handouts several times greater than what the Cambodians earn. Strong Buddhist traditions have taught the Cambodians to make due and be happy with what they have. It was not uncommon to see five people (parents and three kids) on a scooter; 30 people riding in or on a pickup truck; or a family of four living in a lean-to made of scrap lumber and sheet metal, cooking their meal over a fire fueled by someone else's garbage. Some were also making do with what they didn't have, especially the many land mine amputees playing in music bands for spare change, including one band on the Siam Reap Bar Street that was selling their music on CD.

Because of the Khmer Rouge, the better part of an entire generation is missing, and the kids, matured dozens of years beyond their age, are picking up the slack. In and around Siam Reap I saw two dusty boys, maybe 10 years old, walking down the street with bulging burlap bags slung over their shoulders and serious, 40-year-old looks on their faces; a little girl, no more than 9 years old, caring for her toddler sister; another little girl, maybe seven, preparing a meal; a boy who might have been 10 years old, tending to his family's flock of goats; and a 12-year-old boy taking care of the family cow. When not doing their chores, the kids were being kids, playing and splashing in their local swimming holes to beat the tropical heat; running around their homes; napping in hammocks; or playing in the roads. In every instance, their parents were nowhere to be found.

The rest of the kids were at the tourist attractions begging for money or selling postcards, trinkets, bottled water, or knock-off versions of the most popular books at the time. At one temple, a 10-year-old girl selling postcards followed me into the ruins. Working hard to sell me the cards, she counted to ten in English, German, French, Italian, Spanish, Japanese, and Mandarin. If the kids were lucky, their adult handlers – usually not their parents – might give them a paltry cut of the total proceeds. When I first entered the Banteay Srei ruins, 23 miles outside of Siam Reap, there was a little girl, maybe 7 years old, in a red, white and blue-striped rugby shirt just inside the ruins, carrying a notebook with a blue cover. She looked at me, but wouldn't smile or speak when I said "hello" to her. When I reached the back of the ruins about an hour later, she suddenly appeared and handed me a picture of a flower she drew in her notebook with a green ball-point pen. When I took the drawing, I saw a Cambodian man, her handler, standing 20 feet behind her and watching us. I found a dollar in my backpack, folded it tight, casually moved close to her and, out of view of the man, slipped the money into her hand. When I walked away after she let me take her photo, I looked back to see her run around the corner, jump up, and give me a wide toothy smile and a big, thankful wave.

There's no doubt that Cambodia is full of little heartbreakers desperate to earn some money to help their parents feed their families, but this is absolutely no reason to prey on them for sex. Cambodia is one of the world's top destinations for pedophiles. Prevalent are advertisements warning adults to keep away from the kids; and for legit tourists and hotel employees to report any suspicious activities. Violators will get at least 20 years in a Cambodian prison before serving jail time in their native countries. When I asked an American teacher friend from the Pacific Northwest who worked in a kindergarten in Siam Reap about the sex tourists, Anne said that she had seen a few questionable Western men who she thought could have been perverts on the prowl. In one Siam Reap tuk-tuk, I saw a pasty white, freckled, and balding Western tourist — who would have been more comfortable in a London pub — in the company of an almost too-young Asian girl slouched way down low in her seat and wearing sunglasses too big for her face. If anyone wants to go to Cambodia to get their freak on, they only need to walk alone after dark along Pokambor Avenue in Siam Reap that runs parallel to the Siam Reap River, or stroll through the park in front of the U.S. Embassy in Phnom Penh after sunset, where the lady boys of legal age are cruising for customers. Just keep in mind that Cambodia has one of the highest HIV/AIDS infection rates in the world.

The hot Cambodian air, thick with humidity, was clean except for the campfire smoke from the cooking fires, and the sunny blue sky was a nice change from China. But more often than not, the country's water was poisonous. A canal of black raw sewage flowed through Siam Reap and emptied into the Siam Reap River. Raw sewage bubbled up into the street near my Phnom Penh hotel, and flowed next to where people pitched a tent made of scrap wood and sheet plastic on the sidewalk. If the streets in Siam Reap had storm drains to keep the streets from flooding and filling up with mud during every heavy rain, I'm sure they too would have spewed forth some sort of black, smelly nastiness.

The main attraction in Cambodia is the 12th-century temple complex of Angkor just outside Siam Reap. As for Angkor Wat itself – believed to be the largest religious structure in the world – I found it overrated, probably because of its lack of nooks and crannies begging to be explored. Still, visitors should plan at least three days to see the entire Angkor temple complex at a casual pace. Angkor Thom and the Bayon Temple, with its 216 carved faces looking down from every direction on the visitors below, are gems within the overall complex that are worth more than cursory visits.

The highlight of my trip to Angkor was Ta Prohm. Ta Prohm is an excellent example of what happens when someone doesn't mow the lawn for a very long time. Many people may have never heard of Ta Prohm by name, but have seen it in the movie "Tomb Raider" starring Angelina Jolie as adventure hottie Lara Croft. I don't know how long Angelina stayed in Siam Reap, but she sure did leave an impression. At Ta Prohm there is one tree known as "The Tomb Raider Tree" that was featured in the movie; and the drink list in any Siam Reap watering hole isn't complete without the "Tomb Raider", a unique concoction of Cointreau, lime juice, and tonic water. Ta Prohm wasn't my favorite place because of Angelina Jolie (I never saw the movie), but because I'm a big fan of Mother Nature when she shows us mere humans who's the boss. Nothing gets the adrenaline going like a good electrical storm, blizzard, ice storm, etc., that can, in an instant, send modern-day society back to the eighteenth century. Maybe this finally explains my fascination with the Weather Channel, when after all these years I thought it was weather cutie Jill Brown who, in the early 1990s, put the wind in my sails.

I visited Cambodia during the rainy season, and most of the country was under water and being used to grow rice. It seemed like the only dry ground was the 30-foot wide and 200-mile-long ribbon of national highway, NH6, between Siam Reap and Phnom Penh. Each side of the road was lined with houses on stilts, goats, cows, and water buffalo all competing for the same meager grass; while cars, scooters, motorcycles, tuk-tuks, buses, trucks, bicycles, pedestrians, you name it traveling in both directions competed for their share of asphalt. Phnom Penh, the largest city in Cambodia, is a six-hour, $10 bus ride from Siam Reap. Being the capital city, it has a greater number of foreigners, a larger number of adorable street kids, and seemingly more Cadillac Escalades per capita than any other city in the world. Phnom Penh also has what must be one of the largest U.S. embassies in the world, although I'm not sure why the U.S. government requires such a massive outpost in this otherwise simple country. Phnom Penh, after one long day of sightseeing, reminded me of Athens and Bangkok: a must-see place, but where one should not spend more than two days before making their way to the nicer, more interesting destinations deserving of a much longer stay.

As advertised at all the tourist attractions, foreigners will pay more for some things than the Cambodians, but I never had the impression that the Cambodians were trying to rip me off. Maybe it was the Chinese cabbies that made me think that the Cambodian taxi and tuk-tuk drivers were land sharks, but they are benign, non-threatening, willing to negotiate, and happy to help the wayward tourist. When I landed in Siam Reap, one tuk-tuk driver – for a dollar – let me borrow his cell phone to call my hotel to fix a minor problem. The only person who genuinely tried to rip me off was Roberta, a grandmotherly American living in Phnom Penh who was selling what appeared to be locally-made "Obama/Biden" campaign pins for $5.00 each (with no mention of the proceeds going to the Obama/Biden campaign) at an expat event replaying the Biden/Palin vice-presidential debate in a Phnom Penh restaurant central to the Western expat community. Apparently her social security check didn't go that far in Cambodia either.

Given that just thirty years ago, some two million Cambodians, or one-fifth the total population, were killed by civil war, genocide, and the resultant disease and famine, Cambodia has come a long way in a short time. Knowing where their bread is buttered, Cambodian schools now require students to learn English and Mandarin. Cambodia still relies on billions of dollars in foreign aid (a Japanese storm sewer project in Phnom Penh; United Nations activities all across the country; private donors from the U.S., U.K., Canada, and elsewhere funding house and school construction; Koreans and Indians funding the restoration of ancient ruins) but things are looking up. From 2004-2007, GDP growth exceeded 10 percent per year, slowed down to 6.7 percent in 2008, declined by two percent in 2009 during the Great Recession, rebounded to six percent in 2010, increased by 7.8 percent in 2011, and was forecasted to grow by 6.2 percent in 2012.[66] To parlay this growth into bigger things, the Cambodian government during the summer of 2011 opened the Cambodian Securities Exchange (CSX) which has one listed company, the Phnom Penh Water Supply Authority. On my pre-dawn drive to the Phnom Penh International Airport to head back to China, my driver pointed to the hundreds of people out for their daily exercise, doing their best to stay in shape before the sun became too hot. He mentioned that this was a good sign for Cambodia because the people we saw now had a reason to exercise.

Whenever I recommend to people that they should put Cambodia on their must-see list, their initial expression is that of a wrinkled nose and a doubting eye. But no one should let a "yuck factor" keep them away from exploring this most amazing country.

---

66 www.eicambodia.com

CHAPTER 19

PRIVILEGE HAS ITS PRICE TAG

AFTER MY FIRST YEAR OF LIVING AND WORKING IN DÀLIÁN, I WAS FINALLY getting into my groove. So much so, I bought some plants to decorate my new fifth-floor apartment a couple blocks from the old Japanese Imperial Headquarters for Manchuria, and shopped for a makeshift wine refrigerator to store the stash my coworkers brought over from the U.S. This was a big change from my 28th-floor, formaldehyde-contaminated, and nomad-centric apartment which was, for all intents and purposes, a white-walled concrete box with a couch, a TV, and a bed. My first apartment was so sterile and depressing that some of my Chinese friends didn't like to visit me. I sensed that these minor improvements to the quality of my living space signified that I had a new-found sense of normalcy. The icing on the cake was when I signed up to run the Běijīng International Half Marathon on October 19, 2009. I had been looking for some sort of normalcy and the semblance of a routine for a few years – one reason I moved to China was to travel less – and there was no better indicator for normalcy than finding the time to train for a half-marathon. Well, I thought I was living a normal existence until it was time to pay the race registration fee…

When I'm in the U.S., I am just another Middle Class Joe, indistinguishable from the other tens of millions of Middle Class

Joes. On my drive to work, the roads are full of middle-class cars going to middle-class jobs. A morning stop at Starbucks for an extra boost means standing in a long line of khaki-clad, middle-class caffeine junkies looking for their first fix of the morning, each of them known by the barista who calls out their drink of choice before they get a chance to order. During the day, I would look around and see hundreds of other non-descript white collar workers, knowing that we all shared a similar language and a similar profile. At the end of each day, the roads were once again filled with middle-class cars full of said non-descript middle-class Joes and Jills, most of whom were heading home to their spouse and their 2.1 kids. I was just another face in the crowd; another brick in the wall.

However, in China in 2008, where the average annual income for city-dweller was approximately $2,000 per year, and less than half that in the countryside, Joe and Jill Middle Class jump right into the ranks of China's privileged class. Having a car and driver only reinforced the perception. Westerners look different than the Chinese, so we tended to stick out in a crowd and take on a type of rock star status. This is especially true the further one travels from Shànghǎi and Běijīng. Sometimes rock stars can be scary, as I found out on one of at least a half-dozen trips to the city of Héngshuǐ (衡水), population 460,240, in Héběi Province where I made a little kid cry because he'd never before seen a white guy, let alone a 6-foot-4 white guy pushing 190 pounds. With this new found status comes some responsibility (maybe I shouldn't have tried to scare the locals when I went into the countryside), lest one foreigner gives the rest a bad name.

Of course, each individual is responsible for how they handle their new socioeconomic status. As any prescription painkiller addict will tell you, there is a fine line that distinguishes use from abuse. One time while in the Shànghǎi Pǔdōng International Airport on a return trip to Dàlián, I was discussing this very topic with my fellow travelers: one Chinese guy and the Indian guy who accompanied me to Switzerland. I proved my point by using the First Class/VIP security line although I had a coach class ticket just like the other two. When I handed the security officer my passport and boarding pass, he did his usual check and let me through without any hassle. I then had to wait five minutes for the other two to clear security. In Dàlián, like many Chinese airports whose size cannot keep up with the demand for air travel, passengers are sometimes bused from the plane on the tarmac to the arrival gate in either the First Class short bus, or the economy-class sardine-can big bus. When flying in China, I made a point to sit two rows behind First Class so I could deplane and walk onto the much nicer First Class Bus, since the Chinese believe that no self-respecting foreign business traveler would even consider flying economy. I boarded the First Class Bus like I owned it, said hello to the bus driver in Mandarin, and I was never refused entry. Over time, as I realized I'd gone from use to abuse of my whiteness, I opted to play by the rules.

On occasion, people have told me that my face could stop traffic, so I decided to put it to the test. On my commute home each evening, Wáng and I passed by a very wide spot in the road where there once was a set of toll booths, and where the Chinese didn't hesitate to turn three lanes into nine and sometimes ten lanes of traffic. The only problem is that the laws of physics still applied when the wide spot ended a couple hundred yards later and the nine lanes had to squeeze back down into three. Once in a while a car tried to fight us for space and came within a few inches of reconfirming those laws of physics. That's when I would roll down my tinted window so the driver could see my white face. Once they saw that they were going up against a foreigner, they usually backed off to give us the right of way.

In addition to stopping traffic, I was also able to make it flow once again. During one morning commute, Wáng was waved to the side of the road by a traffic cop. Not sure why, I just sat quietly in the front seat of the car like I did every day. Wáng stepped out of the car, went over to the policeman, and pointed toward me. When the policeman saw my white face, he let us go. On another occasion when Wáng was fighting for priority on a crowded street in downtown Dàlián, I asked him to roll down his window. I then said to the other driver and passenger, in Chinese, "where are you going?" Probably more shocked to hear Chinese coming from the mouth of a white guy, they froze for a split second, which was plenty of time for Wáng to jump ahead of them.

This wasn't limited to Dàlián where Westerners were, at the time, still a novelty. One time in the parking lot of a Shànghǎi sports arena, Chén, my Shànghǎi driver, was driving to the place where my coworkers and I played in an expat softball league. The parking attendant was clearly pissed when Chén ignored him — drivers tend to take on an air of invincibility when their charge is a foreigner — and yelled at Chén to stop. We stopped and Chén rolled down my window to talk with the attendant. When the attendant saw me, his anger instantly turned into a wide smile of teeth stained brown with tobacco and wide gaps where the teeth just gave up, and he waved us on to where we were already headed.

But just because I'm a foreigner doesn't mean that everyone is going bend the rules for me. After becoming over-confident in my whiteness, I tried to take eight small items through the "five items or less" lane at a Dàlián Carrefour. Even after trying my best All-American White Boy smile, the cashier sent me packing to the longer lines with my eight items. All the rules in China are pretty much negotiable except at the Carrefour, but I still consider myself quite fortunate when people choose to flex them for my benefit.

Of course, with the good comes the bad because privilege has its price. First there is the lack of privacy. In China, there are 2.6 billion eyes and ears, and absolutely no secrets. It was where I could finally say that Britney Spears and I had something in common. This could just be part of the Chinese culture, but sometimes I felt as if I was Mr. Anderson (aka Neo) living in The

Matrix. Wáng's cell phone was crammed with the phone numbers of almost all the Chinese people I encountered, including my landlord, Chinese teacher, coworker's drivers, relocation assistants, housekeeper, Chinese coworkers, etc. When I needed something done, I briefly mentioned it to Wáng and things were fixed with minimal effort on my part. But things started getting a little weird and uncomfortable when the Chinese not in my primary social circle approached and addressed me with the familiarity of a long-lost friend. I once walked into the Starbucks in my new neighborhood and one girl behind the counter called me by name even though I never talked with her before. When I asked her how she knew my name, she became circumspect and found a reason to focus on her work. At another Starbucks, the girl behind the counter told me all about one of my coworkers, their wife, kids, and their coffee-drinking habits. I'll also never forget the time, a month or two after moving to Dàlián, when one of my American coworkers called to tell me that Freddy the doorman at one of Dàlián's five-star hotels had just told him that I was in my 30s and single, and that Freddy wanted to set me up with Lucy the door girl. At various other social events in Dàlián where there was a mix of Chinese business types, foreign expats, the occasional foreign diplomat or Chinese government official, it was not uncommon to have Chinese people who I didn't know call me out by my first name as they approached me to engage in some friendly chit-chat. These encounters usually involved them asking me questions. When I started asking them questions, they too found a reason to disappear.

Then there's the truly unwanted attention. This comes from not only a steady stream of hookers, beggars, and touts, but from the regular Chinese people too. In April 2008, after a day of sightseeing in the ancient city of Píngyáo in quiet Shānxī Province, my friends from Portland and I stopped to have a beer on an outdoor porch along one of the main streets lined with hostels and restaurants. While we sat there enjoying the peace and quiet during the remaining hour of sunlight, at least a dozen people thought we were interesting enough to photograph, so started snapping pix at will without asking. At first it was a bit of a novelty, but by the tenth tourist, I started calling out to the photographers in Mandarin: "You want our photograph? You give us money! 100 RMB [$14 at the time]!" As we sat there, the price slowly crept to 1000 RMB, and we all – Chinese tourists included – had a good laugh. A few years earlier when I was sightseeing in a temple in Shànghǎi, a Chinese girl suddenly grabbed me by the arm and spun me around as if we were square dancing to face her friend who was waiting with her camera at the ready. Of course, all of this pales in comparison to my coworker who the Chinese thought looked like David Beckham, his pretty blonde wife, and their four pretty, yellow-haired kids ranging from 3 to 13 years old at the time. When they first arrived in Dàlián and walked down the street, everyone wanted a photo with the blonde family; pet the youngest girl's head; and handed their diaperless babies to their very-surprised 13-year-old daughter for a photo op. After the first couple of weeks of their two-year assignment, they pretty much stopped walking around town. I guess the attention was probably one reason they eventually moved to Utah.

The other price to be paid is just that: money. Gone were the days of the separate Chinese and foreigner menus where the foreigner prices were double or triple those paid by the locals, but it is still commonplace for foreigners to be charged higher prices than the locals. (In fairness to the Chinese, there's a diner just off of I-5 in Oregon on the California-Oregon border that's rumored to have separate menus with different pricing for the locals and those just passing through.) China is a shining example of laissez faire capitalism at its best. If foreigners can understand some Chinese, they're already smarter than the first-timers just off the plane, and can save themselves some money. On my first trip to Běijīng in October 2004, I paid my cabbie around 285 RMB to get to my hotel, but now I have the fare down to 70-80 RMB to the exact same hotel from the exact same airport. During my first business trip to Dàlián in March 2007, I started getting hungry while out exploring the city. When I stopped to buy a banana, I asked the vendor in Chinese, "How much for one banana?" He replied, "2 RMB ($0.25 at the time)." I then said to him, "In Shànghǎi, one banana costs 1 RMB, so why is it 2 RMB here?" When his wife who was sitting behind him started to laugh, he knew he could only accept 1 RMB. I know that a single RMB was still quite expensive for one banana, but it was easier to deal in single RMB increments than smaller change. In October 2006, in a taxi from the Shànghǎi Pǔdōng Airport to my hotel, the cab fare for a ride that usually costs about 170 RMB depending on traffic came to around 388 RMB. My cabbie settled for the 150 RMB after I told him that I would not get out of his taxi until he accepted my offer. In February 2008 when I was exiting the Běijīng Subway, I heard a woman yelling in Mandarin, *Dìtú, yī kuài!* (块)![67] (地图一块!, Map, one kuai!) As I turned the corner, the woman saw me, and the next words out of her mouth were, in very clear English, "Would you like to buy a map? Two RMB." I just stayed silent and went on my way.

But with a little strategy, it's possible for foreigners to pay closer to the local price. On many occasions in Dàlián, Wáng would accompany me to a market where I would show him the specific item I wanted to buy. We would separate to different parts of the market, he would head to another stall that sold the same item, negotiate down to the local price, and pay for the item. We would regroup beyond the sight of the stall where he bought the item, and I'd pay him back when we got to the car. To some this would be a hassle, but for us it turned into a game of scamming the scammers.

One time when a few of us expats were talking about our Chinese travels, a Chinese coworker chimed in to tell us about his

---

67   "kuài" is slang term for one RMB.

recent trip to the Forbidden City in Běijīng: the ticket price in English was listed as 60 RMB, but the price was listed in Chinese as 40 RMB. In November 2008 when I was in Běijīng with my sister, I saw the same sign. I asked for two tickets and was charged 40 RMB per ticket probably because I asked for the tickets in Mandarin. By September 2009, a trip to the Forbidden City cost the same 60 RMB for both Mandarin speakers and English speakers, and in October 2011 the fees were still the same 60 RMB. If the Chinese were up-front about the fee schedule – in Cambodia, all fees are clearly listed in English, and foreigners are told that they will pay more than the locals – then it would have been less of an issue, but the rub came when they tried to take advantage of the unwitting foreigner by placing a 40 RMB charge in the English translation for an automatic guide that is not listed in the Chinese version of the sign, giving the foreigner the impression that, since 40 RMB is listed in both translations, the translations were equivalent.

All this talk about overpricing in Běijīng brings me back to the Běijīng Half-Marathon that I thought would bring my life a greater sense of normalcy. The entry fee for Chinese nationals was 100 RMB ($14.64 at the time), while that for a foreigner was $100 (683.20 RMB at the time). A 683 percent markup was definitely not the 50 percent markup to enter the Forbidden City or the 100 percent markup for the tourist map or banana, but at least the race organizers were upfront about it. Of course, I didn't have to pay and didn't have to run, but that would have denied me of my sense of normalcy. Then again, maybe my whole China adventure has redefined "normalcy" to now include incessant overpricing and unwanted attention that came with my supposed rock star lifestyle. If my life in China was any indication of how Britney, Brad, J Lo , Angelina, Paris, Lindsay, and anyone with the last name Kardashian gets by each day, then I now know why I've tried so hard all these years to not become rich and famous. Privilege, of course, has its perks and bonuses, but sometimes the price tag can be just a bit too high.

CHAPTER 20

YOU SMELL SOMETHING?

As part of my foreign assignment, language lessons were made available to me and my non-Chinese coworkers. In China, especially in Dàlián, language lessons were not just a fluffy expat perk, but a true necessity for daily survival. My lessons were straight from a book, and my teacher and I followed the book pretty well. Once in a while, to spice things up, we digressed from the book so Maggie could teach me some common phrases and sayings the Chinese like to use, as well as a bit about modern Chinese culture. During one lesson, Maggie started talking about expressions the Chinese sometimes use in the event of sensory overload. That is, when someone is at a dinner and faced with a wide variety of flavorful food choices, that person is said to have *kǒufú* (口福, pronounced "co-foo") which means "mouth blessing" or "fortunate mouth". When one hears very good music or pleasing sounds, that person is said to have *ěrfú* (耳福, pronounced "R-foo") which means "ear blessing". So goes the same for sight. When a person is faced with a most beautiful vision, scenery, etc., they are said to have *yǎnfú* (眼福) which, of course, means "eye blessing". Being an engineer, it only seemed logical to extrapolate the entomology to include another one of the five senses. When I asked Maggie about *bífú* (鼻福, pronounced "bee-foo") or "nose blessing", she laughed out loud and said, "There's no such thing as *bìfù*! Chinese people don't say *bìfù*!" Having lived in China for the better part of two years by the time this conversation occurred, I really should have known better than to ask the question in the first place.

A day in Dàlián didn't go by without a hodge-podge of foul-smelling experiences. If it wasn't the flavors emanating from the manhole covers on the city sewers, or the sulfur-laden coal smoke from one of the half-dozen power plants I passed by on my 20-mile commute to the office, then it was the industrial solvents that were coming from what must have been the world's largest magic marker factory upwind of the highway, or the thick black smoke belching from the nearby petrochemical plant flare stacks that burned like birthday candles on steroids. Of course, there were the classic smells that became part of the normal landscape: cigarette smoke, body odor, rotten garbage, some coworker's left-over fish dinner being heated in the microwave; whatever was being served in the office cafeteria; diesel exhaust, eye-burning ammonia from not-so-clean toilets; sour shit found in the trash cans next to said not-so-clean toilets where used toilet paper was tossed because many plumbing systems couldn't handle the paper; and clouds of stale bad breath so thick that they lingered in elevators well after the occupants had left. And that was before lunch. The other half of the day consisted of more of the same, but usually with some mothballs (used in urinals as a deodorant); a nasty aliphatic organic (toxic, I'm sure) industrial solvent found in oil- and lead-based paints and floor waxes. It's been said[68] that humans can identify about 10,000 odors, but I guess those researchers never traveled to China.

The human olfactory membrane, which gives people their sense of smell, is approximately one-inch long and located high up in the nasal cavity. In this olfactory membrane, there are about 12 million olfactory receptor cells, which translate into an olfactory

68   http://serendip.brynmawr.edu/bb/neuro/neuro00/web2/lto.html

surface area of 1.5 square inches.[69] This may seem like a lot, but it's a mere speck when compared to a bloodhound's four *billion* olfactory cells that cover an astonishing 59 square inches. Besides having a smaller olfactory region than bloodhounds, people have developed a powerful mechanism in the brain to suppress conscious recognition of an odor. This suppression mechanism allows humans to direct their attention to other things such as work, school, and tasks considered necessary for everyday living. Without this mechanism, people would suffer through smell-activated attention deficit disorder (ADD) each time they encountered a new odor. Nothing would get done, and less would get done in China. This ability to suppress a conscious recognition is what distinguishes humans as more intelligent animals, making the Chinese some of the most intelligent people in the world. I can only imagine what China smells like to a bloodhound. This may explain why I never saw one in China: they all went crazy, or they weren't fast enough.

One of the challenges I had as a native of a clean-air country living in China was expecting the Chinese to validate my question, "What's that smell?" Having been born and raised without "nose blessing", the Chinese have a higher tolerance to odors than foreigners. One day at the office, I walked into a room and smelled the smoke of a wood or paper fire. Since anything is possible on a construction site, and fires are a bad thing during construction, I called over an American coworker for a second opinion. I didn't even have to mention anything because he knew right away why I called him. We then called over a Chinese coworker who said he didn't smell anything unusual (it turned out that the wood smoke from a neighbor that had been drawn in through the air conditioning system). I faced the same challenge when I tried to get someone to find and fix the odors coming into my first Dàlián apartment. For whatever reason, the air pressure in my apartment

69   http://faculty.washington.edu/chudler/facts.html

went negative to the building, and the cooking and cigarette smells from the 27 floors below were sucked into my apartment through what was supposed to be an exhaust duct. It wasn't until the odors almost made me nauseous before a Chinese friend finally understood what I was talking about. Maybe the Chinese do have the same sense of smell as us clean-air natives, but have effectively burned out their olfactory cells with the smoke of the two trillion cigarettes smoked annually. If people are going out of their way to suck in concentrated cigarette smoke, then a smelly toilet, sewer gas, or bad breath, in the big scheme of things, really aren't that bad. Maybe this is why so many Chinese people smoke. For years I tried to persuade my friend Romuald to quit smoking, but while we were living and working in Israel in 1997, I encouraged him to light up at just the right time during our daily commute past a sewer treatment facility which was nothing more than a pond of decomposing raw sewage.

Speaking of sewer gas, it is very common in China to have it emanating from the floor drains and sinks because there are no p-traps. P-traps are those curvy pieces of pipe under your sink that trap a little bit of water to form a seal to keep the nasty gases out. The $1.00 p-traps are required by Chinese building code but to save cost they just aren't installed. It was common to get a good whiff of nastiness at various times during the day, or all day during the summer months when the bacteria grew the fastest, depending on when and what people were flushing down their toilets. Of course, that's if the residence had a toilet. In some parts around Dàlián, toilets are just holes in a piece of concrete over an open ditch running alongside the road; or in some cases, the patch of dirt next to a crowded sidewalk, or the closest tree.

I've become a true believer in the law of averages. After experiencing much *bìfù* in my lifetime − fresh cut grass in the countryside; my mother's Sunday roast beef dinner on a cold winter day; pine trees after a summer rain; campfire smoke; fresh-baked chocolate chip cookies; a crisp autumn day hiking in the

Adirondack Mountains; Estee Lauder's *Beautiful* and Burberry's *London* reminding me of happier albeit short-lived times – it was just a matter of time before the real bad ones came along with my Chinese assignment.

The smell of death isn't new to me. During my redneck days in Massena, I experienced this smell in the form of a flattened raccoon or skunk in the road. The good thing about these was that the smell extended to only a few hundred feet to each side of the mess. In Dàlián, however, the smell of death took on greater proportions in frequency and magnitude. During the summer, a day didn't pass without experiencing the smell of rancid seafood and shellfish. The rancid seafood smell in Dàlián was like none I have experienced anywhere else in the world. It came from the giant piles of rotting seashells that were leftover from the seasonal harvest that occurred in the fishing villages along the coastline; and from what I was told was a fish food factory that used dead fish to make food for the live fish, the piscine equivalent of a cattle rendering plant. As the heat and humidity spiked during the summer months, square miles around Dàlián smelled like rancid fish. It was not just a fleeting odor, but it was a thick, dense, lingering stench of death. Once inhaled, it took a few minutes, if lucky, to dilute itself off the taste buds and the olfactory membrane. If unfortunate commuters were too late to roll up their windows, then a palatable cloud of rot stayed in the car for hours unless it was chased out by rolling down their windows in a fresher pocket of air, if one could be found. The stink permeated car upholstery and clothing, and persisted for days. Some days it was so strong and thick that gagging was the only natural reaction. Whenever I had a first-time visitor to Dàlián in my car, I made a point to open the car windows at just the right time during the commute to the office so I could share my pain.

And this pain was my pain because all the Chinese were going about their daily business as if nothing was wrong, abnormal, or incredibly smelly. Part of this had to do with the innate ability of the Chinese to not show displeasure in miserable situations; and part had to do with the ability of the Chinese, after a lifetime of practice, to tolerate adverse conditions. In all honesty, the rancid dead fish smell wasn't as bad the second summer in Dàlián as it was during my first summer, and by the third, nothing really seemed out of the ordinary. That scared me because it meant that I was getting used to the smells. Actually, the longer I stayed in China, the overall smelliness of the place seemed to decline, which meant either my olfactory membrane was down to 10 million active cells, or I was becoming more intelligent. I guess it's true that if something doesn't kill you, it will make you stronger.

Now that I've returned to the clean-air world, there are times when I think back and miss the olfactory smorgasbord that China threw in my face. It was the raw China, the real China, and an integral part of the whole China experience. Looking back, I wouldn't have had it any other way. If you're just starting out on your first Chinese adventure, you need to remember only one thing: something doesn't smell really bad until you see a Chinese person holding their nose.

CHAPTER 21

FLAT STANLEY DOES DĀNDŌNG (丹东)

WHEN I WAS IN DÀLIÁN, MY COUSIN IN TEXAS ASKED ME IF I WOULD BE interested in helping her husband's then seven-year-old niece Gillian with a school project involving a character known as Flat Stanley.[70] He's flat because he's a piece of paper that the kids put in the mail to distant places to learn about the culture and the people who live in those places. Always trying to be a good sport, I didn't hesitate to help. In February 2009, I took Stanley to up to Dāndōng, China, a small city along the west side of the Yālù (鸭绿) River that forms part of the border between China and North Korea. When it came time to return Flat Stanley to Texas, I realized that the kids weren't the only ones getting an education from this project: I've done my fair share of writing over the years to a wide variety of audiences, but I've never written a letter to third graders. I had no idea how to do it. I struggled through a brief letter, leaving out many good details. After I put Stanley, some photographs and the letter in the mail, I felt compelled to rewrite Stanley's letter as it should have been written in the first place:

"Hi boys and girls! I'm just back from Dàlián and Dāndōng, China, and let me tell you something: it was pretty fucking cold

---

70   http://www.flatstanley.com/

up there! (Ok kids, first lesson: 'fuck' is an integral, necessary, very important, and versatile word in the English language, so ask your teacher to explain all forms of it to you.) There was definitely some brass monkey weather going on in those parts. During winter you're better off staying in Texas. Dàlián was an okay place, but you will find it really boring. There was nothing very interesting for third graders to see in Dàlián except for some smoky power plants, a couple polluted beaches, and a lot of stinky places. Places like Dàlián are important in this world because they make Texas and Mississippi look like great places to live. I really couldn't complain too much about Dàlián because I met some Chinese cuties that wanted to keep me warm all winter. The last place I expected to get a case of Yellow Fever was in northern China, but the Chinese variant of the disease can be very, very serious. Don't let your daddy's company send him to China alone, lest he get sick with Yellow Fever and kick your mommy out of the house when he returns. I could have spent all my time with the girls embracing the local culture, but I wanted to do some other types of exploring to maximize my cultural experience. So, when I heard my friend John was going to Dāndōng, I decided to go north to see what that place was all about. Dāndōng is about a two-hour drive north of Dàlián if you break the speed limit the entire way, with only farm-land and a 100-acre, kick-ass furniture factory – one that probably stole your neighbor's daddy's job – between the two.

"The Boy Scout motto is 'Always be Prepared'. So, like any good Boy Scout, I had to prepare for my trip to Dāndōng by going to the supermarket to buy a 25-kilogram (55-pound) bag of rice. The word on the street in Dàlián was that a 25-kilogram bag of rice will buy a North Korean wife. You see, there is no food in North Korea because the North Korean leader and his friends are spending all the country's money on nuclear bombs and expensive whiskey rather than on fertilizer and seeds to grow food. The North Korean people are very, very poor and very, very hungry because they have not had a good food harvest for a couple of years. Winters are very, very cold, and many people – especially the Korean third-graders and their grandparents – will die if they don't get any food. Since Korean girls are very pretty, and a 25-kilogram bag of rice is priceless to starving people, some girls did whatever it took to feed their families. I'm just not so sure a North Korean girl would be hot-to-trot for a white guy much skinnier and shorter than she. I guess it all depends on how hungry her family, and how lonely she, really is. So, just remember this you little fuckers: when your parents, oh, I meant Santa, doesn't buy you a Wii, an iPhone, or an iPad this Christmas because your father lost his $50/hour union job at the car factory, don't go bawling your eyes out or bitching to anyone about how poor your family is because there are some little boys and girls just like you in North Korea who don't have an older sister anymore because she sold herself to some Chinese guy for a fucking bag of rice.

"Dāndōng has 600,000 people. That's a shitload of people, but Dāndōng is a small city by Chinese standards. The primary attraction in Dāndōng, besides finding a North Korean wife, is to look at North Korea on the other side of the river. Even though Dāndōng is China's largest exporter of toilet seats to Wal-Mart,[71] there's fuck-all to do, so people go to Dāndōng just to look across the river. In Dāndōng there are two bridges that cross the river. Well, one and a half bridges: one goes all the way across, and the other one right next to it goes only halfway across because it was bombed by the Americans during what the Chinese call 'The War to Resist U.S. Aggression and Aid Korea', known to most Americans as 'The Korean War'. For 10 RMB ($1.50 at the time), John was able to walk out to the end of the half-bridge. Part of the tour is to look at shrapnel damage to verify the claims that something bad had happened at this location, as if half a bridge didn't tell the story by itself. Kids, can you say 'shrapnel'? When a bomb – like those your Daddy might be dropping on or throwing at the brown people

---

71 McGregor, Richard, *The Party: The Secret World of China's Communist Rulers*, Harper, New York, New York, June 2010.

somewhere in the world right now – explodes, pieces (the shrapnel) from it fly through the air and cut little boys and girls like you in half. But I digress. When I was at the end of the bridge, I looked through binoculars to see young soldiers with guns watching children not much younger than them playing on a sidewalk; people riding bicycles; and others who were walking along the river. All these people seemed to be well-fed and leading normal lives, so they were probably government workers whose job it is to look like they are leading normal lives, if the normal lives involved only well-dressed people walking past an empty amusement park at dead stop next to boats stuck in the mud that looked as if they hadn't floated for years. At night, the Dāndōng side of the bridge that crosses the river was lit up like Las Vegas while the North Korean side was pitch black. That's not fucking normal.

"In Yālù River Park that runs along the Dāndōng side of the river, Chinese people were selling small trinkets, pins with the face of Chairman Mao; counterfeit U.S. money (most likely printed in North Korea) at a crazy exchange rate; and North Korean money that was probably fake. Not many white people visit Dāndōng, so we Americans were more of an attraction than North Korea. The Chinese people kept staring at us. One angry Chinese woman – ok kids, can you say 'angry'? – who wanted to yell at someone about something asked John if he was Russian, and he had to explain to her that he wasn't. She walked on and began to spew her venom at a one-footed beggar sitting on a frozen sidewalk showing everyone his bare stump, telling him he gave Chinese people a bad name. We never learned what the fuck her problem was.

"Dāndōng was also home to The Memorial Hall of the War to Resist U.S. Aggression and Aid Korea, which would seem like an odd place for Americans to visit. It was in this museum where we learned how the 'American Imperialists drew the flames of war to the Yālù River', and how almost one million brave Chinese volunteers helped save Korea, and to push the imperialist dogs back to the 38th parallel. Ok kids, can you say 'Biological Warfare?' The museum also had a display showing how the U.S. military used germ-infected insects and rodents to kill the Chinese and North Koreans. This museum was well worth visiting because many of the displays had English subtitles and a different perspective from what is taught in the U.S. It also had a gift shop that sold coffee cups with the museum name and logo in English and Chinese (a perfect Christmas gift for the Korean War vet in your family); pens made of big bullets; model helicopters and airplanes made of smaller bullets; North Korean cigarettes and liquor; old North Korean postage stamps and money; South Korean chewing gum, potato chips, Ritz cracker look-alikes; and the occasional souvenir picture book. Just outside the museum we made some new Chinese friends. The kids had been visiting the museum with their grandparents, learning about all the bad things your grandparents did to their grandparents in the mountains of Korea. But since all that happened almost 60 years ago, they were happy to pose in a picture with me.

"The death and destruction of war was getting us hungry so we stopped for Korean food for lunch. You see, when the Yālù freezes, it's easy for the North Koreans to escape to China if the North Korean soldiers don't shoot them in the back. Because there are so many North Koreans in Dāndōng, it was easy to find good Korean food. This is like what happens in Texas and Arizona and why it's easy to find good Mexican food, except the Mexicans need to sneak through a desert and worry about being shot in the front. Koreans like to eat kimchi, which are traditional pickled vegetables - mostly cabbage, carrots, and beets - eaten during winter, when there is even less food. Each autumn, vegetables are mixed in a big clay vase with spices and salt water, and then set outside or buried in the back yard for the cold winter months. This gives kimchi a very special taste. When hungry, they dig up the pot and grab a quick snack. If there is no vegetable harvest, then they're really fucked. Koreans also like to eat a specialty that is called gǒu ròu (狗肉), pronounced 'go-row' in Chinese, and 'dog meat' in English. *Gǒu ròu* should not be mixed up with *rè gǒu* (热狗), pronounced 'ruh-gou', and means "hot dog" in English, but I'm sure the workers at every hot dog factory in the world mix them up quite often. If you were wondering, dog meat tastes like roasted pork, but is much fattier. When John realized how much fat there was on roasted dog, he made a mental note to call his mother to see if hers had gone missing.

"Just north of Dāndōng is the easternmost part of the Great Wall, which is considered by some people to be one of the Seven Wonders of the World, right up there with 'how the fuck did George W. Bush get elected for a second term?' Ok boys and girls, what the fuck was that all about? Built between 500 BC and 1600 AD, the Great Wall of China is a shining example of why people shouldn't fuck with the Chinese when they get motivated to do something. Originally built to keep out the Mongol invaders, this short piece of renovated wall runs along the China-North Korean border and it wasn't clear who was being kept in or out.

"The North Korean border – a simple fence that could be easily climbed by those fast enough – was less than 100 feet away on the other side of a small stream next to the Great Wall. While there, two North Korean soldiers on patrol on this quiet stretch of border started talking to us in Korean and Chinese but we ignored them. They didn't want their picture taken with me, but John took one anyhow. Just then, a spooky guy in plain clothes with a cell phone came out of nowhere on the Chinese side of the border, and the three of them talked about us in Chinese, trying to figure out our nationality. By this time it was getting dark and time to get the fuck out of Dodge and to head back to Dàlián.

"So kids, there you have it. I hope you have learned something today besides how to pick your nose in class. Just remember that you have a good thing going there in Texas, so don't fuck it up. Your Traveling Friend, Flat Stanley."

CHAPTER 22

FINDING FIJI

THERE I WAS, SITTING AT THE INTERNATIONAL GATES OF THE DÀLIÁN Airport, sipping on an overpriced, mediocre cappuccino waiting for my flight. I was on my way to Fiji but first had to stop at Incheon International Airport in Korea to meet up with a Chinese friend from Běijīng. All I had with me was a simple carry-on bag of gear, 817 Chinese RMB, 100 U.S. dollars, 300 Russian Rubles, and a credit card. I left my Filipino, Singaporean, and Malaysian currency at home since, I thought, it wouldn't be exchangeable because all the people who live in those countries already had their own tropical islands on which to vacation. After seeing a large number of Russians in Sānyà, I figured the Russians would be taking their oil money to Fiji too and I could finally get rid of the rubles at an exchange counter.

One could be forgiven for thinking something improper or suspicious was in the works, but the first reality was that it was the start of the 2009 Chinese Lunar New Year holiday. It was once again that time of year when the entire Chinese population jams onto limited numbers of trains, planes, and automobiles — making this annual event one of the world's largest shifts of humanity — to head home to see their families and to give it their best effort to blow themselves up with fireworks (remember kids, fireworks

are all fun and games until someone loses an eye). This Spring Festival was quite the misnomer because it occurred in late January when the Siberian winds passing through Dàlián cut like a knife. Going tropical was a no-brainer.

The second reality was that nothing says "vacation destination" more than political unrest, natural disaster, and financial collapse. I learned this firsthand while in Thailand in 1997 during the Asian financial crisis. No one could beat the $250 price tag for seven nights in a Phuket hotel and round-trip airfare from Bangkok to Phuket, all purchased from a five-star hotel travel agent with one-day notice. Fast forward to 2009, and the world was once again on the edge of financial collapse; the Fijian government was still under military rule after a December 2008 coup; and a week before our arrival, tourists couldn't get out of Fiji fast enough to escape Tropical Depression 04F that inundated the city of Nadi, home to the country's international airport, with six feet of water. A budget traveler's trifecta. It couldn't get any better than that...

But that's when our luck started to run out. When I plan a trip, I consider the sights that I want to see, the things there are to do, and what it takes to get to said sights and activities. I'm also a big fan of walking and exploring until my feet hurt, and rubbing elbows with the local people to better understand their culture. But as I kept planning the trip, I realized that I was about to face my second greatest traveling fear: the resort hotel. Don't get me wrong, since

I know that resort hotels play an important service for the elderly and the traveling public that have too much money, too little sense of adventure, and no taste for good food. Every time I think of a resort hotel, I start to hear The Eagles sing "Hotel California". But because we only had a week to explore Fiji, we decided to stay in a resort close to the main island of Viti Levu since it offered the most opportunity to wander to various places. The small islands that make up most of Fiji provide what Fiji is most famous for, but by their very nature are not good for wandering or exploring.

Once settled into the resort, a relatively empty but clean and well-designed property with friendly staff and pristine, air-conditioned rooms, the first thing I wanted to do was escape. A walk down Queens Road, the dusty main drag of Nadi, was a hectic and crowded affair. It was hard to believe that the street was recently a river. The locals were either rebuilding their stores or trying to get the best deals at flood sales at the stores that weren't rebuilding. Those who were not in the stores were on the streets working hard to attract the handful of remaining Western tourists into their trinket shops. Although Nadi is a city with almost 31,000 people, the walk from the north end of Queens Road to the south took a mere 15 minutes. At the north end of Queen's Road, there was nothing except for a pot-holed road that went to the airport, to the resorts, and to what must be the most remote McDonald's restaurant in the world. At the south end of Queens Road, also the south edge of town, was a Hindu temple that looked much better in photographs than in person and could have used a few prayers of its own. Beyond it was nothing but sugar cane and a scattering of dilapidated houses. It had been many years since any queen paid a visit to this particular road. After a quick tour of Nadi, it was clear that: (1) it wasn't somewhere I'd wanted to be after dark, and (2) the tourist dollars were not finding their way into the local economy. Fiji was a good example of how trickle-down economics didn't work like it should.

Two of my expat coworkers from Dàlián also happened to be in Fiji for the same holiday, so the four of us decided to do some exploring farther afield by hiring a car and driver. The road from Nadi to Suva, the nation's capital, was a tattered narrow ribbon of asphalt that was probably easier to navigate than Fiji's tumultuous political history. The road, weaving over mountains, past sugar cane fields, and along the coast, was dotted with signs that said, "The National Speed Limit is 80 km/h." Everyone takes this seriously on and off the road. During the drive I saw a whole lot of people doing a whole lot of not much since there wasn't much to do except watch the rain slowly eat away at the road.

The Fijian rainy season is from November to April, but the rain didn't stop the locals from getting along with their daily activities as if the sun was shining. Some high school kids played rugby in ankle-deep water, people were selling vegetables alongside the road, some other kids were wrestling with their peers; and men in dirty, tattered clothing who walked along the road had clearly been out harvesting coconuts, breadfruit, and other edibles. This may explain why almost all the adult males carried a machete, which seemed to be the implement of choice. But then again, when the *Lonely Planet Fiji Guidebook (7th Edition)*[72] says, "Walking around [Suva] during daylight hours is perfectly safe; however, as soon as night begins to descend it's a no go. From dusk onwards locals are smart enough to catch a taxi, even for a distance of 300 meters..." it made perfect sense carry a little somethin'-somethin' just in case. I was just glad that they weren't carrying cannibal forks. Who said cannibals weren't civilized?

After living in China for over two years, I forgot what it was like to see churches by the roadside. In Fiji, there were plenty: Catholic, Protestant, Muslim, Hindu, Jehovah's Witnesses, and two Mormon boys – in their trademark white shirt, tie, and black shoes who traded in their black pants for black traditional Fijian

---

72   J. Vaisutus, M. Dapin, C. Waddell, V. Jealous, *Lonely Planet Fiji, Seventh Edition,* Lonely Planet Publishing, Footscray,Victoria, Australia

Sulus – going door to door trolling for recruits. Fijians could use all the prayers they could muster. In 2008, the Fijian gross domestic product contracted by 0.1 percent, contracted by 0.3 percent in 2009, and by 2010 it grew by a meager 0.1 percent.[73] Compounding the poverty issues was the spread of disease. According to the February 1, 2009, *Fiji Times*, one woman died of leptospirosis; the number of dengue fever cases was up to 54 from 30 the previous week; and doctors treated six cases of typhoid.

The road to Suva was also littered with billboards advertising resort homes for sale. For $2.5 million, anyone could have their very own tropical paradise surrounded by high concrete walls and a single entrance manned 24 hours by an armed security guard. Take away the yellow paint, tennis court, and palm trees, and I can come up with another name besides "resort". Resort hotels in third-world tropical destinations are pretty much all the same, and Fiji is no exception: self-enclosed compounds where white people manage the brown people who serve the white people and almost all of the profits are funneled out of country to large overseas corporations. Generally, these communities or hotels are located far from anywhere except a local village cobbled together with cinderblocks and sheet metal, and never the two shall meet. Not much had changed in Fiji since its colonial days.

After spending the first couple days exploring Viti Levu, it was easy to see why people don't venture too far outside the resorts. Having lost all my desire to wander, I focused on doing nothing except relaxing in the sun. It was time to accept my fate as a resort guest, catch up on my reading, and work on my tan. But of course, a trip to Fiji wouldn't be complete without experiencing firsthand the turquoise waters and sandy beaches that everyone knows from the postcards and travel brochures. The quickest way to Fiji's more picturesque locales is to visit the Mamanucas Group of islands just off the coast of Viti Levu. The high point of the trip

---

73 www.gfmag.com

was a day on the ocean and a half-day visit to Monuriki Island where "Castaway" starring Tom Hanks was filmed. The only catch was that Monuriki is not as isolated as portrayed in movie because it's within cell phone coverage of Viti Levu, and a five-minute boat trip or a 20-minute swim to the kava-infused island village of Yanuya. When I saw the movie, I didn't recall seeing a beach littered with whiskey and beer bottles or balled up dirty diapers. Still, the warm waters were pristine, the salty breeze was fresh, the sun was hot, and we were nowhere near the resort. All was good.

As I sat there like Tom Hanks pondering his rescue, I realized that a trip to Fiji requires at least a month. The ideal vacation: slow island hopping with a backpack, swim trunks, a copy of *War and Peace*, and not a care in the world. If I, for some reason, had to go into hiding, I think I would also put Fiji on my list of places to go. The only thing that would probably be the death of me – if not the typhoid, dengue fever, leptospirosis or cannibals – would be the isolation. About three quarters of the way through the trip, I became conscious of being very far removed from the rest of the world. It was getting on my nerves. I think almost all of it had to do with the monotony of resort living and bumping into the same people every day. After a couple days, with the exception of the military declarations (free elections would not be held for ten years), or deportations (the Australian editor of the *Fiji Times*), one already knew what to expect from Fiji: generally good weather, warm waters, white sandy beaches, palm trees, sugar cane, mosquitoes after dark, fresh fish for dinner. By the seventh day, I couldn't get to the airport fast enough. When looking back, I really couldn't complain because when all was said and done, even though we were stuck in a resort we were still able to experience a few of the many faces that Fiji has to offer. My only regret was that I wasn't able to lose my 300 rubles. With a barrel of crude at the time costing less than a good bottle of wine, it seemed that Russian oil money didn't stretch as far as it once did.

CHAPTER 23

FREEDOM VS. DEMOCRACY

JUST BEFORE THANKSGIVING 2008, AN AMERICAN COWORKER OF MINE was in Dàlián for a business trip. During one morning commute, Val mentioned to me that Guns N' Roses was releasing a new album entitled, *Chinese Democracy*. By this time I had been out of the U.S. long enough to become used to being out of touch, but I was a bit surprised and a little excited to hear this news since I've been a GN'R fan since their *Appetite for Destruction* album. *Chinese Democracy* seemed to be a pretty ballsy album name, and I wasn't too surprised when I heard that it came from Axl Rose. As a dutiful GN'R fan, I surfed the Chinese Internet, poked through the Great Firewall of China, and downloaded the album from an iTunes server in the U.S. just as I did for all my music when I was living and working in China. The only difference was that all the other music I bought was good music. The album sucked. I'm all for ballsy titles, but ballsy titles need to be backed up with ballsy music. The Chinese government originally put up a stink about the album, but I think they eventually realized they shouldn't burn so many calories getting worked up over some crappy music. In January 2009, just to say I did, I overpaid for a copy of *Chinese Democracy* in a Shànghǎi music shop that was selling the CD for the equivalent of $2.94.

With the 2008 Běijīng Olympics and controversial torch run around the world fresh in everyone's mind, it probably made sense for GN'R to use the title *Chinese Democracy* as a ploy to sell more albums by leveraging that anti-China sentiment. If I had to pick a word to describe the album title, it would be "overcompensate", like a fat, middle-aged bald guy trying to make up for various physical limitations by buying the biggest, baddest, most expensive, flashiest sports car to impress the ladies. Another word that could be used to describe *Chinese Democracy* is "confused". If I had to guess, I would say that GN'R titled their album *Chinese Democracy* in an attempt criticize the freedoms of speech and press as well as other personal freedoms that apparently, from their limited perspective, don't exist in China.

Where the confusion lies is that "democracy" and "freedom" are not interchangeable words. The Merriam Webster Online Dictionary defines "freedom" as "*1: the quality or state of being free:*

as *a: the absence of necessity, coercion, or constraint in choice or action *b: liberation from slavery or restraint or from the power of another: independence *c: the quality or state of being exempt or released usually from something onerous <freedom from care> *d: ease facility <spoke the language with freedom> *e: the quality of being frank, open, or outspoken <answered with freedom> *f: improper familiarity *g: boldness of conception or execution *h: unrestricted use <gave him the freedom of their home>.* "[74]*

In contrast, the same Merriam Webster online dictionary defines "democracy" as, "*1 a: government by the people; especially rule of the majority *b: a government in which the supreme power is vested in the people and exercised by them directly or indirectly through a system of representation usually involving periodically held free elections. 2: a political unit that has a government. 3 capitalized: the principles and policies of the Democratic party in the United States<from emancipation Republicanism to New Deal Democracy -- C. M. Roberts>. 4: the common people especially when constituting the source of political authority. 5: the absence of hereditary or arbitrary class distinctions or privileges.* "[75]*

Personal freedom of choice is a cornerstone to a democracy, but a democracy is not a prerequisite for people to be free. Just because China does not have a democratic form of government doesn't mean that the people in today's China are not free. Because of recent Chinese history, many people outside China believe China is led by a heavy-handed Communist Party that exercises its absolute power to influence all aspects of Chinese society.[76] When one who has never been to China thinks about the Communist Party, they envision a heavy-handed government and a whole population wearing blue or gray Mao suits. But from my experiences, interfacing with the Chinese government (and

---

74 http://www.merriam-webster.com/

75 Ibid.

76 McGregor, Richard, *The Party: The Secret World of China's Communist Rulers*, Harper, New York, New York, June 2010.

---

hence, the Chinese Communist Party) for visa, work permit, and other administrative items was no different than interfacing with the U.S. government when it comes to paying taxes, obtaining a new passport, crossing back into the U.S. after an international trip, etc. Of course, all us expats were all cognizant of the Party and the Government, but we didn't leave our apartments every morning looking over our shoulder or feeling repressed or limited in our thoughts and actions in fear of an authoritarian reprisal. And after years of watching the Chinese people in action, this is how the everyday Chinese people also seem to approach their government. In some respects, it's as if there are two Chinas – those in the Party, and those not – and most of the time, neither the two shall meet unless one upsets the other to the point of soliciting a response. For the rest of the time, so as long as they don't upset each other or the social stability, everyone's pretty much free do whatever the hell they want. When I returned to the U.S. after my first trip to China in September 2003, I told all my friends, "If that was communism, then sign me up!"

Today's China is a very different China than that which existed during Chairman Mao's Great Leap Forward (大跃进, *Dà Yuè Jìn*) from 1958-1960 when millions died of starvation, but it's still a poor and developing country. One of the biggest non-fatal impacts on Chinese society from the chaos resulting from the Great Leap Forward and then the 1967 formation of the Red Guards (红卫兵, *Hóng Wèibīng*) during the Cultural Revolution (文化大革命, *Wénhuà Dàgémìng*) was a total breakdown in the trust between the people and the government. Individuals lost all faith in the government's ability to provide a basic standard of living and, as a result, honed sharp instincts for self-preservation. But this survival instinct seems to have been baked into the Chinese DNA many years prior. In his landmark 1935 book *My Country and My People* (吾国与吾民, *Wú Guó Yǔ Wú Mín*), Lín Yǔtáng (林语堂) wrote that China had become a collection of millions of family units rather than a cohesive society. Lín illustrated this nicely with the image of a handful of sand where the hand symbolizes the Chinese government, and each grain of sand is a family unit. If the sand is thrown to the wind, the family unit remains a unit even though the hand is gone. The individuals outside one's family unit essentially become background noise and a natural force, like the weather, which is tolerated. When looked at through the eyes of Westerners, this gives the impression that the Chinese do not value human life, which I think is the wrong conclusion to draw. The Chinese value their lives and the members of their family unit. A side effect of this family unit mindset is that people are expected to mind their own business and not interfere with things outside their family unit. If someone opts to interfere – such as the woman in Chapter 1 who tried to help the 2-year-old girl run over twice by a car – they are ostracized by others for meddling. After a couple years of living in China, I realized that over time I became increasingly detached from the masses of people around me. If someone wasn't a friend or colleague, or someone I had to interact with for daily survival, then they and the rest were relegated to the status of "background noise" or obstacles that were to be avoided or overcome so I could achieve my objectives. Of course I knew that that the "background noise" was more than just noise and obstacles, but living, breathing people, but my brain classified them not as people, but objects. I realize that this is a harsh thing to say, but it's the truth. Now multiply that attitude by 1.34 billion. In one example in 2007 in Chóngqìng (重庆), China, three people were trampled to death in a mad rush when Carrefour, the French version of Wal-Mart, put cooking oil on sale.

Because they developed their individualistic survival instincts, one could argue that China's citizenry have always been free thinkers even if those thoughts are kept from public consumption. The more public demonstrations of freedom of thought can be found in the exclusive Xīntiāndì neighborhood in Shànghǎi – located on the site of the first meeting of the Chinese Communist

Party – that is considered Ground Zero for Western capitalism in the city; and the 798 Arts District at the site of a former Chinese defense contractor in Běijīng. In fact, during my three and a half years living and working in China, I never met a Chinese person, Communist Party members included, who toed the party line; and those middle class Chinese who I know to be members of the Communist Party are free-thinkers and bigger capitalists than I.

In China, so as long as someone doesn't commit serious crimes, threatens the political and social stability, discusses the Three T's (Tiananmen, Taiwan, and Tibet), preaches religion, or talks smack about the Party, then China is pretty much a free-for-all, or at least it seems that way at the individual, grassroots level. Many may disagree with me, but China is freer than the United States. Too lazy to walk to the toilet? Piss on the street. Need some spare change? Steal a manhole cover and sell it for scrap metal at the same place the driver of the car who hits the uncovered hole at 30 miles per hour will soon take their car. Don't want a speeding or red-light ticket? Remove or cover your license plate numbers so the photo radar cameras can't ID you or doctor the plates so they can't be traced. Want to start a business? Anyone with a means to cook food is an instant street vendor, no permits required, and cooks are not even required to wash their hands after they pick their nose or wipe their ass. Eat off the street, and you might get more than what you bargained for, or something completely different than what you expected.[77] Americans think they're free, but try carrying an opened bottle of beer out of a bar or restaurant and see what happens. In China, nothing happens and the beer doesn't go to waste.

When compared to everyday China, American libertarianism is on par with the Republican Tea Party in Utah. Grassroots Chinese society is libertarianism at its best and its worst. Things start

---

77 I met one Western guy in Shanghai who ate what he thought was beef or lamb from a street vendor, only later to realize that he ended up with a case of worms from what turned out to be rat meat.

to go sour when libertarianism and freedom transition into chaos. For the sake of simplicity, I'll define the start of chaos as the point when blood begins to flow and people begin to die premature and unnatural deaths. Generally speaking, I found that the Chinese tended to resort to violence faster than Western cultures. Based on the carnage I've seen, the arguments and fights I've witnessed, and the stories I've heard, it's not a stretch to conclude that China might be too free. Beer bottles tend to be the weapons of choice to settle arguments in night clubs; and I saw two bloodied men, friends no less, who beat each other up in a restaurant after a drunken argument. After a small fender bender, the driver of one of my coworkers was stabbed in the leg by the other driver, who then ran over my coworker's foot in his escape. On January 8, 2009, a Dàlián man was killed after he was struck by three hit-and-run drivers in less than ten minutes while he tried to cross a road. He tried to get out of the road after the first guy hit him, but never had a chance after the second and third cars hit him. It's not clear if any of the drivers were found. I know of a fight among migrant workers that resulted in a stabbing that put one man in the hospital and another man in jail because of a disagreement over the equivalent of 0.30 Chinese RMB ($0.04 at the time). In May 2009 in Guǎngzhōu, China, a 66-year-old passerby, inconvenienced by a five-hour traffic jam caused by a man threatening to jump from a bridge, broke through the police lines and pushed the jumper off the bridge.[78] The jumper survived. In August 2011 in Shanghai, a crowd gathered not to help but to encourage a 21-year-old college student to jump to her death from her fifth-floor apartment.[79] The *China Daily*, China's national English language newspaper, always runs stories on theft, killings, suicide, and corruption throughout the country. So much so, I refused to show my mother the paper when she visited China lest she worry about my safety.

---

78   http://news.xinhuanet.com/english/2009-05/23/content_11422634.htm
79   http://www.echinacities.com/expat-corner/the-radical-option-psychology-of-suicide-in-china.html

Given that the published stories are meant for consumption by the non-Chinese speaking foreign population, one can only imagine what else is taking place elsewhere in the country.

A Chinese friend from Shànghǎi once asked me, "Do you know why the Chinese government is always encouraging a 'peaceful and harmonious society'?" Before I could give him an answer, he replied, "Because there isn't any." As my reading comprehension of Mandarin improved, I started reading more of the banners and slogans posted around the country. The characters that showed up the most were *wén* (文) and *míng* (明), when placed together as *wén míng* (文明), translate into "civilized" or "civilization". In the men's rooms at the Dàlián International Airport there are signs above the urinals reminding users that "one small step forward is one big step for civilization" to stem the flow of the Yellow River running along the floor; in Jǐnán (济南), there were many *wén míng jiāo tōng* (文明交通), or "civilized traffic" signs posted around the city; in Xiàmén (厦门), there was a sign encouraging people to be more civilized; in Xī'ān (西安) there were plenty of signs encouraging civilized language, *wén míng yǔ* (文明语), etc. There are so many *wén míng* signs posted across China that they have become cliché. When I asked a Chinese friend in Dàlián why there were so many *wén míng* signs, he gave me the typical Chinese response: a shrug, a brief pause, and then a terse "I don't know." Although my friend wouldn't answer the question, I already knew the answer: because there isn't any.

"And because there isn't any" is a big reason why the Chinese government is doing what they're doing. There is not another government in the history of the world that has ever faced the challenges that now confront the Chinese government, and no one is giving the Chinese much credit for what they're trying to do or what they've already accomplished. There are more people in China today than there were in the entire world in 1800; and China is only 300 million people shy of the global population in 1900. Sure, the Chinese have some interesting boundary conditions with respect to public gatherings, religion, internet access, etc., but one must understand the context in which these conditions are set: social stability. The Chinese government was criticized in 2009-2010 by many people around the world when they imposed martial law in Urumqi in Xīnjiāng (新疆) Province after tensions between the Uighur (pronounced "WEE-gur") population and the Han Chinese flared up into fatal violence. In retrospect, the Chinese did what they had to do for two reasons: (1) to stop the immediate bloodshed and to keep it from escalating; and (2) to send a message to the other minority groups that may consider following in the footsteps of the handful of Uighur and Han Chinese who started the conflagration in the first place. If any of the ethnic minorities among the 55 minority groups officially recognized by the Chinese Central government were given special treatment after a spate of violence, then all the other ethnic minorities would be incentivized to resort to the same type of violence. That could feasibly turn into a mass uprising of at least 100 million people. That would be bad. It was in the best interest of the Chinese people for the government to react the way they did in Xīnjiāng. Sure, depending on whom you talk with, the means and methods may not have been perfect, but no system of government can claim to be perfect. Don't forget that it was the democratic process set forth by the U.S. Constitution that enables the ultra-democracy practiced in California in the form of referendum ballot measures and recalls that turned the state into the most dysfunctional in the U.S.

Every person I encounter describes their very first trip to China in the exact same way: China was absolutely nothing like what they expected. In reality, the Chinese people are no different than American people. They all want the same things: a happy and healthy life, a good job, food, clean water, shelter, and personal security. It's just that the Chinese go about it in a slightly different way than Americans. Unfortunately, GN'R won't get a chance to experience this since they pretty much ruined any opportunity they might have had of obtaining Chinese visas. Given all the traveling they did during their *Appetite for Destruction* and *Use Your Illusion* tours, Axl and company should have tried for a couple tour dates in China. If they did, it might have given them the inspiration to give their latest album a more China-appropriate title that worked quite well for them in the past: "Welcome to the Jungle".

CHAPTER 24

BURMESE DAYS

SUNLIGHT WAS A COUPLE HOURS AWAY AND WE STILL HAD THE ELEMENT of surprise when our small wooden boat pushed off in the quiet morning. The cool breeze along the shore carried with it the fresh, earthy notes from a nearby swamp and an occasional U.S. Constitution that enabled hint of a distant campfire. When we hit deeper waters the motor coughed to life and the gentle breeze against my face turned into a steady cold gust as we headed toward our objective. Any pre-mission jitters were suddenly frozen away as the barrel of my 12-gauge became much colder to the touch. As we bounced over the waves, the tug of my ammo-filled pockets told me that going into the drink wouldn't be a good way to start the day. The duck population on the St. Lawrence River had no idea what was headed their way...

...but the duck population on idyllic Inle Lake in Shan State in northeastern Myanmar was safe for another day. When I opened my eyes I was half a world away, 26 years older and sitting in yet another small wooden boat. The only differences were that I was packing travel gear rather than heat and the boat driver wasn't my father but Ko, a short, deeply tanned and pudgy lake native from the Intha tribe. After a few restful days on the lake, I was heading back to Yangon (Rangoon) where I started my Burmese adventure

two weeks prior. In 1984, I don't think I had even heard of Rangoon or Burma except in history books, and the names "Yangon" and "Myanmar" were not yet part of my vocabulary. Myanmar was never on my list of places to visit, but those two weeks now rank as one of my Top Five all-time trips.

Like Cambodia and Laos, Myanmar has a "yuck factor" associated with it. Not helping matters were the economic sanctions imposed by the European Union and the United States. The whole military dictatorship thing can be a real downer too, but that has recently given way to a civilian government that is heavily influenced by the military. *Lonely Planet* spends several pages debating the ethics of visiting Myanmar, but honestly, if they didn't want anyone to go they wouldn't be selling a $25 book about the place. On the upside, the sanctions have slowed globalization, and it was quite easy to make it through a day without seeing more than a few foreigners. That was a good thing because my flight from

Guǎngzhōu to Yangon was packed with French vacationers who made the Chinese fliers look downright civilized.

Some friends who visited before me described Myanmar as, "India without all the people" and "North Korea without the nukes." I haven't been to India and only briefly stepped foot into North Korea, so I didn't have much on which to base their comparisons. But given the number of ethnic Indians in Yangon and Mandalay, and the number of circa 1960 cars and buses barely held together with the dirt in which they were coated, I can see how easy it would be to make such statements. I found much more than what those statements imply.

There's something wild and exotic about the name "Rangoon" as the Brits called Yangon when Burma was a British colony. Maybe this is because it almost rhymes with "baboon", or maybe because Rudyard Kipling wrote part of *The Jungle Book* in Rangoon. According to the February 19, 2010 edition of the *Economist*, the World Bank some fifty years ago listed Burma as one of Asia's most promising prospects for economic growth. Today, Yangon is a tired and chaotic affair that had seen better days. Vestiges of a more affluent and intellectual past can be gleaned from frequent references to Mr. Kipling; visits to the Savoy and Strand hotels; a mix of left- and right-drive cars driving on the right side of the road; and a downtown area with a thriving and substantial Little India. But times have changed. The Grand Hotel was anything but; the Happy World Amusement Park wasn't; and most of the colonial architecture, with the help of high-sulfur diesel exhaust that choked many streets, was dissolving into its natural state. Poverty was commonplace, but like Cambodia, I saw little misery. There wasn't a time when I felt unsafe. The biggest risk to personal safety after dark was accidentally falling into an open sewer. But like Phnom Penh, Yangon was good for a couple of days before it was time to explore farther afield.

There's a little pucker factor that comes with flying domestic airlines in third world countries that happen to be under economic sanctions that make spare plane parts hard to come by. But flying for twenty minutes in a circa-1980s Fokker 100 still beat an eight-hour, 150 km (93-mile) drive. The only difference was that the Burmese flying experience wasn't as polished. It was necessary to reconfirm flights the day before departure; stickers on passengers' chests indicated airline and destination; paper tickets were the norm; computers were non-existent; security was spotty; and identification was not required. On the plus side, the Air Bagan flight attendants were hot, giving the Thai Airlines and maybe even the Singapore Airlines girls a run for their money.

When I landed in Bagan in February 2009, it hadn't rained since October. The cool, dry mornings were a pleasant switch from soupy Yangon. Bagan is an enjoyable rural escape to the simple life, and is famous for its 4,000-plus stupas dating back to the eleventh century that are scattered across an area about the size of Manhattan. Some were built by kings to honor the Buddha, and others by private citizens hoping to expedite their journey to Nirvana. The oldest and tallest temples that see a steady stream of visitors reach over a hundred feet high and were built without cement or mortar, just gravity and tightly-packed bricks. Now that's faith.

I sensed that, at least in Bagan, Myanmar was longing for its colonial days. At my hotel overlooking the Irrawaddy River, brown people waited on the white people. In the hotel bar, each table held a small service bell that one had to pick up and ring if they wanted to order. While hiding out from the hottest part of the day next to the pool, I saw a scene that could have easily been lifted out of George Orwell's soap opera *Burmese Days* or E.M. Forster's ultimate snoozer, *A Passage to India*: a short parade consisting of elderly white people with mops of white hair, each with a brown man one step behind them, holding an umbrella to protect their pasty-skinned guests from the scorching sun. The few society Brits lounging and chatting by the pool made the time warp seem that much more real. Things must be bad if the native people are longing for the return of the British Empire.

When I arrived in Mandalay, with its one million people and ten traffic lights that sometimes worked, I sensed that I was closing in on my own passage to India as the demographic turned darker and Hindu temples became more pronounced. While Yangon has been the debatable political capital since former dictator General Than Shwe declared Naypyidaw as the new capital, the 151-year-old Mandalay, the last royal capital of Burma, is considered to be the country's commercial engine, which has much to do with Mandalay's proximity to the Chinese border. The sprawling city is a municipal impossibility given the lack of basic infrastructure, but everyone seems to make it work. Most people cooked by campfires that filled the air with thick pungent smoke; and many still manually hauled water out of neighborhood wells rather than turning a tap. Electrical transformers with questionable connections well past their prime crackled with inefficiency, and it was common to see a deadly rat's nest of random wires, in an effort to steal unmetered electricity, slung onto the main power mains that ran overhead. Sewage trickled into the nearest gutters or streets and eventually became rivers of nastiness. Home life seamlessly overflowed onto the sidewalks a couple times each day when the power went out. One typical Mandalay street scene consisted of a woman bathing, another woman tending her house, someone running a small shop, and a makeshift restaurant serving dinner to a handful of patrons, all within 50 feet of each other.

Mandalay won't win any awards for city planning, but the world can learn a little something from it when it comes to tolerance and diversity. On one street I spotted a Catholic church across the street from a Buddhist temple, both about fifty meters (150 feet) down the street from a local mosque, and all were a few blocks over from a Hindu temple. It was one happy neighborhood where everyone lived in peace. Elsewhere in town there was a Baptist church, and even a place for the Mormons to do their thing, which, of course, didn't involve drinking. That's unfortunate because Mandalay is the home of Spirulina Beer, the anti-aging beer. Young forever, baby! Ponce de Leon, eat your heart out.

If you run out of money while drinking yourself young, then you're fucked. Because of the economic sanctions, ATMs were nonexistent and very few hotels take credit cards. Cash is king, as long as it is recently-printed U.S. currency in perfect condition without any folds, creases, tears, or markings not put there by the U.S. Mint. By contrast, the national currency (Kyat) barely held itself together and I was afraid to touch it for fear of catching something or because it would disintegrate in my hands. At Amarapura, the site of the world's longest teak wood bridge just outside of Mandalay, one local woman kept begging me to buy from her two bracelets made from watermelon seeds. All I had were two tired $1.00 bills rejected by others, so I negotiated the bracelets down to $1.00 and gave her the choice of which bill she wanted. She paused, looked them over carefully, and finally made

her choice, probably betting that she could pass it on to some hapless tourist. It just went to show that beggars can be choosers.

As in Cambodia, the Burmese children matured unnecessarily quickly and usually for the wrong reasons. At Inle Lake, youngsters took matters into their own hands and rowed themselves to school in the family boat. At one temple in Bagan, I met three skinny eleven-year-old girls, faces dusted with thanakha,[80] each caring for their one-year-old brothers while their parents were nowhere to be found. One of the two fifteen-year-old boys who became my tour guide in Bagan quit school because his father died and he now had to help his mother pay school fees for his younger siblings. This same boy, when I told him the name of my hotel, said to me, "the pool is very nice. My foreign friend invited me to go swimming." The boy then volunteered, "He also invited me to spend the night in his room, but I got nervous and went back to my village."

Stepping into any Burmese village is like time warping back to a time earlier than even the British Empire. Sandy footpaths that doubled as gutters and storm sewers were the norm; all huts were built on stilts. Women beat the dirt out of the laundry with sticks and stones; fields were plowed by oxen or by hand; and people watered their buffalo. Each village specialized in making a single type of product: lacquerware, gold and silver jewelry, woven baskets, dried fish, blacksmith goods, carvings or furniture, and handwoven fabrics made of cotton, silk, or lotus thread, sand paintings, etc., and every hut in the village was a makeshift workshop.

But while the people were busy making ends meet with their homegrown industries, the government was out to crush its opponents and those "acting as stooges...of external elements" as I saw advertised on a government poster in Mandalay. But the everyday people and the local monks didn't seem to mind having foreigners around. Everywhere I went I was greeted with smiles and friendly waves from passersby, even those who were not trying to sell me

---

80   Bark from the thanakha tree that is ground into a powder and used by the Burmese as a cosmetic and sunblock.

something. "Hello!" was shouted at me at least 20 times daily. The local people, most of who were just trying to make ends meet, were legitimately happy to see strangers wandering around their country. In the big scheme of things, the military government didn't seem to be an issue for the everyday people because the everyday people didn't seem to care. It just goes to show that politics tend to be the concern of those who feel they have something to lose.

When I first wrote this chapter as a blog post in February 2010, I said that "if the rumblings and rumors in the Burmese foreigner circles were true, then things in Myanmar are about to change. As the story went in the foreigner circles, economics Nobel laureate Joseph Stieglitz, commissioned by the Obama Administration and the European Union, visited Myanmar to see if the sanctions imposed on Myanmar were effective in producing their desired results. As the rumor went, he apparently discovered what any visitor will soon notice: the sanctions are hurting the everyday people and not the government, and the sanctions would officially be lifted after the 2010 Myanmar presidential election." On January 13, 2012, better late than never, the U.S. started to normalize economic and diplomatic relations with Myanmar. Progress toward improved trade may take time as supply chains are established, but they've already had a head start: Jim Beam and Bud already figured out how to jump the border while Johnnie's been walking across it for years; Coke products are commonplace in all the high-end hotels; and I started every morning with a bowl of Kellogg's cereal. It just went to show that as long as Myanmar shares borders with China and Thailand, and maintains close relations with Singapore, there will never really be economic sanctions.

Myanmar is a must-see for anyone planning on spending time in Southeast Asia. But see it soon, because this fascinating piece of land that time forgot will soon fall victim to all the good and bad that globalization has to offer.

CHAPTER 25

TRAVELING THE SILK ROAD

UP TO THE LAST DAY OF OUR TRIP, NINA AND I WERE STILL DEBATING about whether or not we entered Tajikistan. We knew that at one point we were only 60 miles from Pakistan and 40 miles from Afghanistan, but for our entire trip we couldn't figure out whether or not we crossed into Tajikistan. We passed through a military checkpoint that required a passport check, but there were no flags or such on the other side of the checkpoint to indicate that we entered another country. Because border areas in remote locations sometimes tend to be a little blurry, I was convinced we had wandered into Tajikistan because we made a stop by Lake Karakul. According to *Lonely Planet*[81] and *Encyclopedia Britannica*[82] Lake Karakul is located in Tajikistan. Nina, a Han Chinese girl in her late twenties, was convinced otherwise, and insisted that we never crossed into Tajikistan. By the end of our trip, we did agree on one thing: Kashgar (known to the Chinese as Kāshí, 喀什) is in Xīnjiāng Province in China, but we were never really sure if we ever were in China.

---

81 http://www.lonelyplanet.com/maps/asia/tajikistan/
82 http://www.britannica.com/EBchecked/topic/312088/Lake-Karakul

---

A Silk Road outpost in the Taklamakan Desert with a history spanning over 2,000 years, the oasis town of Kashgar is the westernmost city in China. It's a place where, as one Chinese saying goes, the mountains are high and the emperor is far away. We were so far west some of the Chinese were white and looked as if they just flew in from Dublin. Unlike most of the rest of China where the Han Chinese are the dominant race and culture, Kashgar and Xīnjiāng Province are dominated by the Uighur people and a Central Asian culture steeped in Islamic traditions. Knowing I was heading into a predominately Muslim region, I took a tip from Nick Danziger[83] and stopped shaving prior to the trip. My clothes gave me away as a Western tourist, but I was much closer to blending in than Nina, the daily target of hundreds of piercing stares and double takes. That is, until we stepped into the

---

83   http://www.amazon.com/Danzigers-Travels-Nick-Danziger/dp/0246130253

modern downtown areas of Kashgar where the Han Chinese were predominant and the Uighur people were far and few between. Where I completely blended in, though, was with my grasp of Mandarin since the Uighurs and I were able to easily understand each other's bad Mandarin while Nina struggled to communicate with them in her native language. I could have busted out the Arabic I remembered, but since I couldn't figure out how to make a meaningful sentence from the words for "water", "God willing", and the c-word (not "cancer"), it was in my best interest to keep my mouth shut. Anyone planning on traveling to China to learn Mandarin shouldn't study in Kashgar. Then again, they shouldn't go there to study Arabic either since the Uighurs speak a Turkic language that is written with Arabic script.

Muslims worldwide are getting a bad rap these days because of the misdeeds of relatively few extremists, but there is something to be said for the sense of community that a religion can bring to a group of people. The streets in Old Kashgar were crowded with vendors, scooters, cars, and at one point a stray flock of sheep, but they were quiet and the people respected each other's space and pace. Pushing and shoving was nonexistent, and people politely yielded to others. Drivers didn't threaten pedestrians, no one tried to rush anyone, cabbies were honest and the taxis were clean. Neighbors talked and everyone seemed to be friendly toward each other. Like I saw in Cambodia and Myanmar, kids barely out of diapers were the accompanying adults for kids still in diapers. Although I saw *wén míng* signs in Kashgar, this was the first Chinese city I've been to where the prevailing vibe was that of civility. Even Nina thought the Uighur people were a breath of fresh air from the Han Chinese. Several times a day we caught ourselves saying, "When we get back to China..." but the occasional loogie launcher and sidewalk driver gave us a jarring reality check.

Old Kashgar, with its narrow, winding alleys and mud brick buildings, has been a trading town for thousands of years, and the variety of shops in Old Town keeps the rich tradition alive. Religious hats, prayer rugs, handmade knives of all sizes, furs, carpets, Xīnjiāng and Iranian saffron, and counterfeit US$100 bills were on offer. So were currencies from just about every country that uses Arabic script, including Iraq and Iran, which allowed me to round out my Axis of Evil currency collection, having bought my North Korean currency in Dāndōng. Shops and sidewalk space doubled as the workshops where goods are still made by hand. Small poplar logs by the hundreds were turned into rolling pins and other baking implements by dozens of woodsmiths around town. So many, in fact, it wasn't clear how many rolling pins one small city required. Blacksmiths still used elbow grease to make horseshoes and copper cookware could be fashioned while you wait. Visitors walking around town will hear a cacophony of hammers on copper, tin, and aluminum while the high-pitched twang of Uighur music emanates from the music shops where instruments were made. With my digital camera it was easy to shoot black and white photos that looked as if they were taken a century ago. For trivia buffs out there, Kashgar was the on-location setting for 1960s Afghanistan in the 2007 movie *The Kite Runner* because Afghanistan was deemed unsafe for filming.

As we strolled through markets crowded with pious men in caps and women covered from head to toe, I felt as if I had been transported back to my days in the Middle East. With cumin, cardamom, barbequed lamb, and the smoke from wood-fired bread ovens wafting on the cool desert breeze, I couldn't help but reminisce about the days I spent wandering the Old City of Jerusalem, the Muslim quarter of Akko, and the Jordanian city of Aqaba. At one point I started craving olives, hummus and Turkish coffee, but then realized I was still in China. It's unfortunate that Old Town Kashgar and its collection of mud brick buildings is getting smaller each day, succumbing to the elements and the wrecking ball as the Chinese central government pushes to modernize and civilize the city with high-rise apartments.

When people or places are in the furthest orbit or at the ends of the spectrum, they tend to get a little quirky. The American Tea

Party movement and Nancy Pelosi come to mind. Kashgar, with a dentist office or two on every city block, is no exception. It was impossible to walk down a street without seeing a sign or a dental chair parked next to the window, giving all pedestrians a front row view into a gaping mouth undergoing a cleaning, an extraction, or a noisy drilling. Dentists were the Kashgar equivalent of psychics in Sedona, Arizona.[84] On some streets, there were three or four dentist offices in a row. There were probably just as many dentist offices as there were nan (bread) shops, explaining the need for so many dentists. To my delight, Kashgar was a Karen Carpenter Free Zone but the trade-off was Elvis. Ablimit "Elvis" Ghopor[85] is a friendly Uighur fluent in English and who has been a tour guide and carpet dealer in Kashgar for over a dozen years. If you want some local help in getting around, or want to shop for carpets, then consider finding Elvis. Even if you don't actively seek him, he'll still find you. Elvis and I traded email before I landed in Kashgar, and before we could set up a meeting time, we, almost too conveniently, bumped into each other on a crowded market street in Old Kashgar.

The shops in Old Town had plenty of wares to offer, but the icing on the cake was the Sunday Market, one of the oldest, biggest, and best in Central Asia. A trip to Kashgar isn't complete without a trip to Sunday Market. The market is open every day, but it's on Sunday when all of Central Asia shows up. Thousands of people and their asses were asses to elbows browsing the fresh meat, vegetables, nuts, candies, spices, clothing, household products, stationary, plumbing supplies, more carpets, lumber, shoes, tourist trinkets, musical instruments, manhole covers, furs and fur hats, and anything that can be transported using a donkey cart. The only odd part of it all was that I didn't see any silk. Outside the

84 According to one Sedona, AZ, resident, there were more psychics in Sedona prior to the Great Recession. Apparently those who closed up shop and moved on didn't see it coming.

85 elvisablimit@yahoo.com; http://www.elvisablimit.jozan.net

market was a Kashgari traffic jam of donkeys, horses, cars, food vendors and others all hodge-podged together, trying their best to occupy the same space at the same time, once again reminding us that China wasn't too far away.

The only thing missing from the Sunday Market were the animals for sale. There was once a time when the Sunday Animal Market and the Sunday Market were all one giant, smelly, messy, chaotic venue so it's probably a good thing they've been separated. We knew we were getting close to the Sunday Animal Market in the southeast part of town when we suddenly saw everyone out for a stroll with their sheep, goats, and cows, and all heading toward the same spot: a dusty lot of several acres, littered with manure of all shapes and sizes. When we entered, hundreds of Uighur men were in deep negotiations while others and their sons, emulating their fathers, wandered through the herds of sheep to probe and check on their teeth, wool, and reproductive potential. Toddlers slept in backs of trucks, some boys chased down a few creatures that tried to make a break for it, and others helped their mothers with the shearing duties. It was easy to see how someone might have mistaken the place for the world's largest petting zoo, but at one point I walked passed a tidy row of freshly severed sheep heads for sale. Masking the smell of the manure in the yard was that of barbequed mutton, making me wonder what the sheep in the field had thought about their entire situation.

Kashgar was good enough for a few days of thorough exploring before things started getting redundant. To break things up, Nina and I headed down the Karakoram Highway to the Lake Karakul we hotly debated, and then onto Tashkurgan, the last Chinese town before the Pakistani border. Like Kashgar, there was nothing along the Karakoram Highway that was remotely similar to the eastern China we left behind. The flawless blue skies and bright sunshine of Xīnjiāng Province was the stuff of hopeful computer renditions posted on billboards in front of property development projects elsewhere in China. At night, the stars were closer and more plentiful than I saw anywhere else in China. The Milky Way was so bright we confused it with a passing cloud.

The Karakoram Highway is a two-lane road that peaks out at around 12,000 feet above sea level and rates as the highest paved international road, and one of the most scenic highways, in the world. On the west side of highway, the rocky foothills of the Pamir Mountain range were tiger-striped with recent snow. To the east were the glacier-covered Kongur and Muztagh-Ata Mountains, the 37th and 43rd highest mountains in the world. As we traveled south, the Pamir Plateau gave way to wide open grassy pastures dotted with boxy mud brick homes, and grazing yak, cows, camels, and sheep. It was impossible to grasp the vastness of the plains and the size of the mountains until we spotted a black speck in the distance that turned out to be a solitary farmer. The silence was deafening.

The town of Tashkurgan, population 28,000, would make a good sister city for Fort Collins, Colorado. Just as Fort Collins has the Front Range of the Rockies to its west, Tashkurgan has the snow-capped Pamir Range to its west. With a town center consisting primarily of an empty traffic circle, hardly a building over two stories, and streets lined with a variety of shops, Tashkurgan could probably pass as Fort Collins about 100 years ago. Just like Fort Collins was a stopping point on the Overland Trail, Tashkurgan is a stopover for those navigating the Khunjerab Pass at the Chinese-Pakistani border. Tashkurgan also has a Wild West frontier town feel to it, and I wouldn't have been surprised to see a good old-fashioned shootout just like in the American Wild West, with the AK-47 taking the place of the six-shooter. Also like Fort Collins, Tashkurgan is a predominately white population, but of Tajik descent. With a little more tan and a set of locally-styled clothes, I could have blended in with the townspeople as long as I kept my mouth shut. It was in Tashkurgan that I learned two things: (1) I found yet another place to go into hiding, if the need should ever arise, and (2) even Marco Polo would have been impressed with the length of Proctor and Gamble's supply chain: Crest toothpaste and Head & Shoulders shampoo were on sale in the local supermarkets.

Looking back, the Tajiks in Tashkurgan were the closest we came to Tajikistan. The border was ten miles due west of Tashkurgan, and according to my GPS (38° 45.00' 5.30" N, 75° 1.00' 13.90" E), the closest we came to the border was about six miles. There happens to be two lakes named Karakul: the biggest one is in Tajikistan and the most famous one is in China. When I returned to Dàlián, I raved to anyone who would listen to me about my most amazing trip. The Han Chinese seemed a little concerned about my safety ("Taliban" was one word I heard repeatedly) and they expressed some skepticism when I suggested that they make a visit. In one way this is good, because that means Kashgar and Tashkurgan will retain its uniqueness, cleanliness, and its culture a little bit longer without suffering total assimilation into the rest of China. In another way it's bad because the Uighurs, Pamir, Kyrgyz, and Tajiks could probably teach the Han Chinese a thing or two about what it means to have a peaceful and harmonious society.

CHAPTER 26

DON'T BE AN EGG

IN MAY 2009, I READ A NEWS REPORT ABOUT MICHAEL HICKS, 55, A contract employee at the IRS office in Detroit, Michigan, who was arrested and convicted of urinating in an elevator. Apparently he had been at it for two years before the Feds finally caught him. In the end, he was fined just over $4,000 for his actions. After I read the story, I said to myself, "What's the big deal?" The IRS is lucky it wasn't something much worse Hicks was leaving in the elevator, or anything I've seen on a regular basis during my travels through China. Maybe this was my first sign that I had been in China a bit too long, or second, after I realized that spitting chicken bones onto my dinner plate doesn't translate well back in the U.S. Unlike some other foreigners I encountered in China, I take pride in consciously making these realizations.

In his most fascinating book, *Us and Them: Understanding Your Tribal Mind*, David Berreby[86] described how cultures of similar people (human kinds) possess an inane ability to understand coded signals via verbal and non-verbal cues each are emitting, allowing members of a particular human kind, even though they

---

86 Berreby, David, *Us and Them: Understanding Your Tribal Mind*, Little, Brown and Company, New York, New York, 2005.

may not know each other personally, to have a basic understanding of each other. It's what allows members of the same culture to "get it". A good example of this would be Asian drivers in the U.S., or U.S. drivers in Asia. Because neither usually understands each other's unspoken rules of the road, accidents occur and tempers flare. During numerous business trips within China to perform supplier quality audits, it was easy to see how companies put the theories in Berreby's book into practice even before the book was published. When I was somewhere out in the provinces, where the last foreigner besides my travel companions was seen a few hours prior, a native Kansan suddenly appeared to explain that it was his job to assure us that everything was under control at the facility. Within minutes, my coworkers and I hit it off with the Kansan, and before we knew it we (Us) were the best of friends, sharing road warrior stories about traveling in China (Them). As it goes with birds of a feather, so it also goes with Westerners in rural China.

As an extension of this strategy, I've had managers at multinational companies with operations in China espouse on numerous occasions about their Western staff who have many years of experience working in China, implying that their company and its people are the best qualified to get things done. These Western staffs are sold by their senior management as the China hands skilled at bridging the Eastern and Western cultures because daily life in China can be a hectic and confusing affair and there is a need for those who can make heads and tails of what many newcomers to China consider semi-controlled chaos. Those who can affect change and be productive in China possess a skill that many others have failed to master. Because of this, bookstores across America are loaded with books about understanding China, and how to do business in China; there are schools such as Portland State University in Portland, Oregon, which offers a master's degree in international management, which is essentially an MBA with a language (Chinese or Japanese) requirement and a focus on Asia. More MBA programs are sending their students to Asia each year, and undergrad study abroad programs are focusing on Asia. Productivity can be a challenge for the Westerner working in China, so it's usually good to work with people and organizations that have some experience in the field to help things go smoothly. Western companies will need more of these people if they want to succeed in the global economy.

By the same token, Westerners new to China can easily fall prey to Berreby's theories on tribal thinking and human types. One may think that being successful in China is about navigating the Chinese, but that's not necessarily the case. It's just as important to know how to navigate the foreigners and when it's best to not follow along with other birds of the same feather. While returning to Dàlián after a visit to Shànghǎi, I walked up to my gate at the airport and saw dozens of Americans sitting in the waiting area. By this time, I had resided in Dàlián for just over a year and I knew that there was absolutely no way all those first-timers to China were going to where I was headed. When they realized that I had been working and living in China, they pelted me with questions about China; I handed out some Imodium (aka "Vitamin I") to an elderly couple who didn't bring any with them; and I taught them the three Chinese phrases – *ní hǎo* (你好, "hello"), *xiè xiè* (谢谢, "thank you") and *wǒ bù yào* (我不要, "I no want") – they would use the most during their whirlwind two-week trip. My flight to Dàlián that evening happened to be called at the same time as their flight to Běijīng, and I started down the escalator to my flight. Right behind me was a woman from the tour group, because on this particular night the Běijīng flight used the same escalator as the Dàlián flight, but a different jet way. Even before I reached the bottom of the escalator and turned toward my plane, I knew what would happen next. As I started walking toward my plane, I turned around to the woman who was now following me and said to her, "You're plane is over there. You don't want to go where I'm going." She seemed a bit confused since I was also a Westerner, but she learned an important lesson about life as a foreigner in China.

While in China, I worked with a few Europeans and Americans who had been in Asia for many years, or rather, too many years. I'll be the first to admit that I fell into Berreby's tribal thinking trap by assuming that their whiteness and their understanding of Western expectations of quality and performance, by definition, held them to the standards that I would expect from any of my American coworkers in the U.S. The catch, as I saw it from my experiences, was that some of those who have stayed too long in Asia have betrayed their whiteness and have become "too Chinese", or at least have assimilated the stereotypical qualities of the Chinese suppliers: short-cutting to save time and money; producing a poor quality product that would require even more time and money to fix or replace; initiating left-field discussions to distract from investigating the root cause of the problem they know they need to fix at their cost; use of delay tactics to answer a question; squeezing every dime until it bleeds to the detriment of a proper long-term strategic solution; fixing the blame for something on everyone except themselves when they're clearly in the wrong; and creating more excuses than a four-year-old caught with their hand in a cookie jar.

I can tolerate this behavior from the native Chinese because it's expected in developing economies, but I have zero tolerance for this type of behavior from the Westerners because I know that they know better. I can say with confidence that I had to watch over some of the Westerners in China with more diligence than the Chinese. These Westerners turned out to be the bigger overall risk because most of them were in senior or executive positions that allowed them to influence or create their corporate policy. They're not looking out for others, only their bottoms and their bottom lines. They may say differently, but their actions spoke louder than their words.

After a few years in China, it was easy to understand how this happens, since it's no different than an experience I had with a general contractor in my hometown a many years ago. The contractor was new to Massena and St. Lawrence County, New York. He came into town with a business model that would have put many others out of business: he would show up to the project, was reasonably priced, and finished the work on time and on budget. The only problem was that after a while, he realized he didn't have to work so hard, and began to pick up the bad habits of the natives. It became impossible for him to finish a job, show up on time, etc. In China, I'm finding that those Westerners who compromise their work ethic are those who realize they don't need to be the best of the best, but only the best of the worst.

Assimilation has been around for as long as people have been traveling. It can be as subtle as preferring green tea to coffee after spending a few years in China, or as extreme as the Borg of *Star Trek* fame where cultural destruction was inevitable and resistance to total assimilation into a homogenous society was futile. Of course, depending on who you talk with, assimilation can be good or bad. Around the same time that Theodore Levitt coined the term "globalization" I was a junior high school social studies student in white bread Massena, learning about the Melting Pot Theory and all its benefits, even though the local population tended toward the NIMBY Theory instead. My June 2008 trip to Běijīng (Chapter 16) made me think twice about the benefits of assimilation and globalization even though I realize it's an inevitable force in the post-modern era.

Ben Franklin said, "Moderation in everything – including moderation." In moderate doses, prescription drugs, scotch, water, hamburgers, vitamins, shredded wheat, and just about everything else, are good things. Too much of a good thing, however, can easily turn into a bad thing. This also applies to assimilation. Unfortunately, there are some who don't realize this, and they are the people whom others, particularly businesspeople new to China, need to be wary. Just because a company may tout the China experience of their

Western employees based in China, or their overall Chinese experience, it doesn't necessarily mean that it's a good thing.

Sure, there are benefits to the cultural assimilation, Melting Pot Theory, etc. that comes with globalization, but don't try telling that to any first generation Indian or Chinese immigrants to the U.S. who refer to their Americanized offspring as coconuts or bananas. Blogger Vijay Prashad[87] wrote, "[The] Indian American coconut, for instance, becomes 'white' in all respects but appearance. The Indian American coconut identifies as white, has 'white tastes' and has a disregard for things Indian." Similarly disparaging opinions can be heard from the Chinese with respect to the first generation ABC's (American-Born Chinese) who are also referred to as "Twinkies" – yellow on the outside, white on the inside. While the Indians have their coconuts, and the Chinese have their bananas and Twinkies, us white boys have our eggs: white on the outside and yellow on the inside. It may be more fitting to call these people *nǎi huáng bāo* (奶黄包) which literally translates into "milk yellow bag" and is a Chinese steamed bun with sweet yellow custard filling on the inside that is usually served at breakfast, but "egg" sounds better and it's easier to remember.

American Miriam Beard, who in 1938 authored the first international cultural history of the businessman, wrote, "Travel is more than the seeing of sights; it is a change that goes on, deep and permanent, in the ideas of living." I'm all about learning from other cultures, but the Melting Pot Theory is too extreme. I'm more a fan of the Alloy Theory whereby the properties and characteristics of a base metal are strengthened by trace amounts of other metals and elements. Stainless steel comes to mind: it starts off as iron, but with a bit of nickel, chromium, molybdenum, manganese, and traces of silicon, sulfur, and phosphorous, it is turned into 316 stainless steel (316SS) where iron is still the primary ingredient. It is possible for Westerners to live in China, learn from the experiences, and enhance and strengthen themselves,

---

87 http:// www.littleindia.com

but too much additive can turn into a contaminant; a vitamin into a poison. Every expat should heed Ben Franklin's advice on moderation and, in short, don't be an egg.

CHAPTER 27

SCARING THE CROWS

DURING MY NORMAL COMMUTE TO WORK FROM DOWNTOWN DÀLIÁN TO the east side of Dàlián's *Kāi Fā Qū*, I usually passed by a small patch of land not far from my office where, in the spring, the local residents planted a variety of crops such as corn, beans, and tomatoes. What piqued my curiosity about this patch of land was that it wasn't your typical flat piece of real estate that someone had to plow, but it was a piece of land at about a 30-degree angle at a tunnel entrance that was paved with hundreds of hollow bricks.

The primary purpose of the hollow bricks is to prevent soil erosion on the hillside at tunnel openings in a way that didn't flood the road. But in this instance they also provided the local residents with hundreds of little flower pots in which to grow fresh vegetables. Arable land in a ten-story apartment building is in short supply, so the locals made best with what was available, rent free, and right outside their front door. It was Chinese innovation at its best. Who else would consider utilizing what is generally considered by many a useless piece of land? I was interested in how the growing season would pan out, so I kept an eye on these gardens each time I passed, surprised that I never saw anyone lying on the sidewalk after a tumble down the hill. Then one day during late summer when the corn was growing

strong, I noticed that a scarecrow fashioned from sticks, rags and plastic bags took up residence in the garden. After three years of living, working, and traveling around China, it was the first scarecrow – *dào cǎo rén* (稻草人), or "rice/paddy grass man" to the Chinese – I ever saw in China. I couldn't help but think back to world renowned sinologist Joseph Needham – the subject of the book *The Man Who Loved China* by Simon Winchester[88]– who started his lifelong research on Chinese culture in the 1940s after noticing that traditional Chinese farming techniques were similar to those of Western cultures. Needham then spent his next 30 years asking, "Who invented it first?" and then answered his own question thousands of times over to formulate his compendium on China. Now it was my turn to ask my own Needham-esqe question: "Who invented the first scarecrow?"

---

88 Winchester, Simon, *The Man Who Loved China: The Fantastic Story of the Eccentric Scientist Who Unlocked the Mysteries of the Middle Kingdom*, Harper, New York, New York, 2008..

For as common as scarecrows are, a complete and detailed scarecrow history is surprisingly hard to find. So, with that said, to start my search I had to turn to a website developed by Mrs. Nelson's third-grade class[89] in Yarmouth, Massachusetts, that reported that the first human-form scarecrow was invented by the Greeks about 2,500 years ago to protect their vineyards from the local bird population. As the mythology goes, Priapus – the incredibly ugly son of Aphrodite[90] and Dionysus[91] – whiled away his days in rural Greece where he spent the better part of his time with farmers who tended to the vineyards. The farmers noticed that when Priapus played among the grapevines, the birds stayed away from the grapes, resulting in some of their best harvests that produced some of their best wine.

For those of you who haven't boned up on your Greek mythology lately, Priapus is not nearly as famous for being the first scarecrow as he is for sporting a giant and permanently erect phallus. So big, in fact, Priapus is said to have once bludgeoned to death a donkey with his tool after the donkey dropped a dime on him while he was sneaking up on a girl who passed out after a couple too many drinks. Of course, it's up to the reader to decide whether it was Priapus' horrific looks, his big boner (who said scarecrows didn't have a brain?) or just the fact that a kid running through the fields kept the birds away from the grapes. In any case, some neighboring farmers carved wooden figures resembling Priapus, placed these figurines in their fields, and hoped for the same results. Just for the record so I don't get her in trouble with the State of Massachusetts, Mrs. Nelson didn't teach her third-grade class about boners. That little tidbit came from the pagans.[92]

Over time, the cultural assimilation thing took over as the Romans learned from the Greeks about the whole scarecrow

---

89 http://home.comcast.net/~minelson/history_of_scarecrows.htm
90 Aphrodite is the Greek goddess of love.
91 Dionysus is the Greek god of the grape harvest, wine making, and wine.
92 http://paganwiccan.about.com/od/mabontheautumnequinox/p/ScareCrows.htm

idea. As the Romans conquered and plundered their way through Europe on their way to England, they brought with them the practice of using scarecrows to protect their crops. Although the Romans never made it as far as Japan, Japanese farmers had their own versions of scarecrows because birds and animals have been eating planted crops for as long as there have been crops. Scarecrows are even mentioned in the Kojiki (古事記, "Record of Ancient Matters"), written in 711-712 and considered the oldest surviving book in Japan.

The Japanese scarecrow, known as Kuebiko, was a god who knew everything about the world, except for how to walk. This is probably one reason why *The Wizard of Oz* is not a Japanese movie. As time went on, it seemed that Kuebiko didn't meet expectations when it came to scaring birds, so the Japanese farmers moved on to various and different things – rags, fish bones, and rancid meat hung from bamboo poles – to protect their crops. These devices were called *kakashi* because they smelled bad ("kaka" apparently being a universal term or prefix for "smelly stuff"). The farmers discovered that kakashi were not too effective either, probably because the stink attracted crows, seagulls, and buzzards all looking for a meal. Not having any luck, the Japanese eventually tried other human forms that didn't stink, but by then the name *kakashi* stuck. According to the pagans,[93] the Japanese would sometimes outfit their stick men with weapons; and in some cases, in lieu of a human form, they mounted rags, noisemakers, and sticks to poles in rice paddies and then lit the whole thing on fire. Boners, weapons, and fires...what more could pagans ask for?

When I started paying more attention to scarecrows, I spotted more around Asia. On one weekend trip to Dāndōng when the corn was nearing harvest, I saw the best-dressed scarecrow in China sporting a silk shirt. In the rural outskirts beyond Mandalay, Myanmar, I saw several scarecrows camping out in a rice

93   Ibid.

paddy; and during a drive from Vientiane to Vang Vieng, Laos, I saw a couple ragged scarecrows watching over a rice harvest. At one point on the road from Vang Vieng to Luang Prabang, I saw what I thought was a scarecrow but turned out to be a girl harvesting rice, albeit at a very slow pace. I doubt she had a boner, but if I was in Thailand instead of Laos, that could have been another story altogether. But I digress...

Employing living people to keep animals from crops goes back hundreds of years. In the Middle Ages, parents in Europe and what is now the United Kingdom who were happy to get their kids out of the house put them to work as scarecrows in much the same way Priapus went about his bird-scaring duties. It was only after the great plague, when there were fewer kids to work the fields, did farmers revert to human-form stick figures. In pre-Columbus North America, Native American men would sit and watch the crops, chasing birds and other animals away as they approached. At first, no one would ever think the Romans had anything in common with the Burmese, but at Myanmar Vineyards in the hills above Inle Lake, Myanmar in February 2010, I saw a young woman walking up and down the dozens of rows of ripened cabernet sauvignon grapes, ringing a bell to keep the birds away.

Scarecrows are known around the world by a wide variety of names such as bogle, flay-crow, mawpin, mawkin, bird-scarer, moggy, shay, guy, bogeyman, shuft, rook-scarer, mommet, murmet, hodmedod, and tattie bogle.[94] The actual term "scarecrow" is believed to have been coined by Daniel Defoe in his 1719 classic *Robinson Crusoe* when Crusoe described how he kept the birds out of his corn crop, saying, "...I could never see a bird near the place as long as my scarecrows hung there...[95]" and some attribute the success of Defoe's novel for the assimilation of the term "scarecrow" into the modern English lexicon.

94 http://en.wikipedia.org/wiki/Scarecrow
95 Defoe, Daniel, *The Life and Adventures of Robinson Crusoe*, Seeley, Service, and Company, Ltd., London, England, 1808.

But that was then, and this is now, and now, harvest is just around the corner depending on which part of the world one lives. And with the harvests, out come the scarecrows. In a bit of quirky assimilation, because harvests in the Northern Hemisphere coincided with Halloween, scarecrows today are generally considered a Halloween symbol, and the scarecrow populations tend to spike in September and October. In Chappell Hill, Texas[96] (pop. 3,000), Marshall, Michigan (pop. 7,500), and St. Charles, Illinois[97] (pop. 31,384), Halloween usually starts around the first weekend of October. In Athens, Tennessee[98] (pop. 14,128) and Bayfield, Wisconsin (pop. 600) usually begins a week later; and apparently Emma Krumbee[99] doesn't have much going on in her life and was looking to juice it up a bit because she starts her Halloween celebration at her apple orchard in Belle Plaine, Minnesota (pop. 4,983) near the beginning of September. If Emma is so hard up for company that she needs to put on a scarecrow festival in September, then she may want to consider becoming a pagan. The more traditional celebrants of Halloween can head to Easton, Pennsylvania (pop. 26,267) where they hold their scarecrow festival as close to October 31 as possible.

If you feel your life isn't complete without having attended at least one scarecrow festival but you don't live in the Northern Hemisphere, then you could head off to Australia for the April-May harvest season. But before you start booking fights and hotels, you had better think again. Even though Australian crops are just being planted in the September-October time frame, the folks Down Under still hold their scarecrow festivals during the Halloween season. If you do happen to be going Down Under, don't forget to check out the Kurrajong Scarecrow Festival,

---

96 http://www.chappellhillmuseum.org/festivals.htm
97 http://www.scarecrowfest.com/
98 http://eventful.com/athens_tn/events/scarecrow-festival-2009-/
E0-001-024953935-5
99 http://www.emmakrumbees.com, really a chain of restaurants in Minnesota/Wisconsin.

Milton Scarecrow Festival, Tamborine Mountain Scarecrow Festival, Middleton County Fair Scarecrow Festival, Maleny Scarecrow Festival, Maffra Scarecrow Festival, Bundanoon Scarecrow Festival, and/or the North Parramatta All Saints Scarecrow Festival.[100] If you completely miss the scarecrow festival boat this year, then mark your calendars now and plan on heading to Wanatah, Indiana (pop. 1,047) next year to see what they'll have on tap. For all you pagans who are planning on attending, please remember that these are all family events.

So, next Halloween, once all the pumpkins have been carved, all the trick-or-treaters have come and gone, and you have completed your annual candy-giving duties, open up a bottle of your favorite wine, pour yourself a glass, and sit back and relax. Before you take your first sip, quietly gaze down into the glass and think back to the inspiration the Greeks received from a similar glass of wine thousands of years prior when they saw Priapus running through the fields. Swirl the nectar around the glass, close your eyes, and take a slow, purposeful sniff to stimulate your taste buds. Take your first sip and let the wine dance across your palate, swishing it with your tongue and allowing its flavors to fill your mouth. As you swallow the wine and savor the finish, open your eyes and be thankful that you or your kids are not so ugly as to inspire your neighbors to create statues in your likeness to scare off the local wildlife.

---

100 http://www.scarecrows-in-motion.com.au/

CHAPTER 28

A ROUNDABOUT APPROACH TO DEMOCRACY

IT WASN'T LONG AFTER I FIRST MOVED TO PORTLAND, OREGON, IN 1993 when I encountered my first traffic circle. If my memory serves me right, I was trying to find a parking place in the Hawthorne District in a neighborhood behind the Bagdad Theatre when I happened upon the circle. It probably wasn't the first traffic circle in my life, but it was the first one that truly left an impression. It wasn't much to write home about because it was just a small spot in the road, but I can still remember thinking about how quaint it seemed. This little spot in the road added to the ambience of the neighborhood of classic, early twentieth century homes and tree-lined streets. It alone probably added five percent to home prices. The world needs more traffic circles and roundabouts. I'm sure the United Kingdom Roundabout Appreciation Society[101] would agree.

Depending on who you ask, the world's first traffic circle was either New York City's Columbus Circle designed in 1904 by William Phelps Eno[102] who was also the inventor of the stop sign and the crosswalk; or the "Carrefour a gyration" in Paris designed in 1906 by Eugène Hénard, the Paris City Architect who is said

---

101 http://www.absoluteastronomy.com/topics/Roundabout_Appreciation_Society
102 http://en.wikipedia.org/wiki/William_Phelps_Eno

to have started thinking about traffic circles as early as 1877.[103] Over time, it was discovered that Eno and Hénard independently arrived at the concept of gyratory traffic movement, but their designs differed by the size of the central island.[104] It seems the British didn't want to be left out of the running for this landmark invention and committed plenty of ink to the June 2008 passing of Frank Blackmore, 98 years old, who was the engineer credited with the invention of the mini-roundabout in 1969.[105]

For the record, there is a difference between a roundabout and a traffic circle. In a roundabout, the cars in the circle have the right of way, while in a traffic circle the cars entering the circle have the right of way. In both cases, these traffic control devices symbolize a passing moment of civility: the ability for two or more people with different goals and ideas to peacefully coexist through compromise. Unlike a stop sign or a traffic light where the driver is given an instruction, traffic circles and roundabouts are generally unlit and sometimes unsigned. The success or failure of these traffic control devices relies completely on the skill and personal characteristics of the drivers passing through them. Almost anyone can obey a stop sign or a red light without thinking. Roundabouts and traffic circles are for the thinking driver who is okay with sharing the road. It shouldn't be a surprise that traffic circles and roundabouts are designed by civil engineers.

Next to sliced bread and the wheel, the traffic circle and roundabout should rank up there as two of the world's best inventions. The circular design with its smooth, efficient curves provides the optimal compromise between stop and go. When traversed correctly, a roundabout harmonizes not only with society, but also with the environment by minimizing gas consumption and giving cities and towns such as Sedona, Arizona – possibly the roundabout capital of the U.S., which might have something to do with

---

103 http://en.wikipedia.org/wiki/Traffic_circle
104 http://www.alaskaroundabouts.com/history.html#history
105 http://www.timesonline.co.uk/tol/comment/obituaries/article4131930.ece

the local energy vortices – a place to plant more trees to absorb some of the carbon dioxide from said cars. The maturity of a particular civilization or society, I'm convinced, can be deduced from the success of traffic circles, roundabouts, and traffic patterns in general. That is, the ease or difficulty of navigating a traffic circle or roundabout in a particular country is directly proportional to that culture's ability and readiness to accept and responsibly practice successful democratic rule. The *Economist* has its Big Mac Index to compare currency valuations in various countries, so it seems that the makings of a "Roundabout Index" to gauge how long until a country is ready for democracy is not too far in the offing.

This brings me to China. In China, traffic circles are wheels of fortune, if they spin at all because the gridlock or fender benders that regularly occur cease all forward movement. The city of Dàlián, unfortunately, is a big fan of roundabouts: Zhōngshān Square (中山广场), Yŏuhăo (Friendship) Square (友好广场), and Găngwān (Harbor) Square (港湾广场) are the most famous, with other unnamed widow-makers scattered throughout the city. The fact that all the traffic circles in the city are named "Square" should also be a warning sign. The Chinese are famed inventors of many things including the compass and toilet paper, but after living in China, I can state with confidence from experience that the traffic circle and roundabout were not Chinese inventions attributed to the French, Brits, or Americans.

On Dàlián's highways of death, there are always traffic police stationed at the roundabouts to help keep things moving, but their efforts are usually futile. In China, roundabouts can be two-way affairs rather than the traditional one-way; and yielding regularly consists of a "fuck the rest of you, I'm going first" attitude with a lot of horn action and then either a close call, fender bender, or a real mess. It's ironic that the French called their first roundabout a "Carrefour a gyration". If they only knew that navigating a Carrefour supermarket in China is no different than navigating a Chinese traffic circle.

Antisocial driving is not solely a Dàlián issue nor a regional Asian issue, but primarily a China issue. Cambodian drivers share the road, and I didn't see one accident in my one week there; after a weeklong trip to the motorcycle-and-scooter-clogged streets of Ho Chi Minh City and a weekend jaunt with plenty of pucker factor out to the Vietnamese coast on country roads, Vietnam seemed relatively accident free;[106] South Korea is so organized and socially considerate that it's boring; ditto with Japan; and Indonesia and the Philippines are good examples of controlled chaos that result in little, if any, damage. During a February 2011 visit to Naga City, Philippines, population 162,313, I couldn't find even one traffic light but the hectic city streets flowed with jeepneys, tuk-tuks, cars, trucks, pedestrians, and motorcycle cabbies, rather than blood, anger, or rage. The Thai drivers pretty much behaved themselves with the exception of a scooter vs. truck fatality I saw on a country road. If the North Koreans could afford cars, I'm confident they would drive like their southern relatives. The two accidents I saw during a two-week visit to Laos each involved a car with Chinese license plates from Yúnnán Province which shares a border with Laos. Upon returning to Dàlián from a trip – any trip – I usually saw at least one accident during what was supposed to be a 15-minute drive from the airport to my apartment.

Many will probably not believe or agree with me, but in some ways today's Chinese society – or the lack thereof – has gone too far down the path to libertarianism to properly instill and foster an effective and successful democratic system based on the rule of law. The late Paul Samuelson, the first American economics Nobel laureate, exclaimed "Libertarianism is its own worst enemy!" when discussing free market economics, but one could argue that this same statement can also apply to politics and very large populations. During my days on a construction site where,

---

106 One friend who spent a couple years living and working in Vietnam told me that he saw plenty of accidents and several of his coworkers arriving at work with some serious road rash; but I saw just one scooter accident while I was there.

at times, over 3,000 migrant workers showed up for work each day, I spent my days reminding almost everyone, for their own benefit, to wear their safety glasses and other personal protective equipment. Each time I would ask someone where their gear as, I received a litany of excuses on par with "the dog ate my home-work." I was talking to grown men and women, but there were many days when I felt like a kindergarten cop.

It's for this reason I have a very high regard for the Chinese leadership. They are facing unprecedented challenges and for many years have been heading into unchartered territory. Multiply those 3,000 construction workers by a factor of 533,333 and that's what the Chinese leaders have to deal with except they're more focused on maintaining social stability, growing the economy, developing infrastructure, feeding their people, trying to keep the melamine out of the milk, ensuring people are adequately and safely housed, attempting to build a social safety net, and cleaning the environment, all the while trying to keep the hot economic growth from burning up the country. Corruption remains a per-sistent issue but is being dealt with on many levels although there are times when the effort seems futile; and the safety and quality of the food supply is improving, but there are still mountains of issues to resolve. Big ships don't turn quickly. With 1.34 billion people, putting something up for a vote may not necessarily be the best for the country whose population can't successfully navi-gate a roundabout or a traffic circle. The year 2012 is not the right time for democracy in China, and there's a good chance that 2013, 2015, or even 2050 won't be the right time either, if ever.

For this reason, to get the ball rolling, it may be time for the Chinese government to consider pulling a page out Rudy Giuliani's playbook for cleaning up New York City. From 1994 to 2001, Rudy bet his success as mayor by relying on the Broken Windows Theory[107] which was later validated by Dutch researchers in 2008:

---

107 http://en.wikipedia.org/wiki/Fixing_Broken_Windows

clean up the nuisances – graffiti, squeegee men, litter, broken windows of abandoned buildings – and bigger societal changes will follow. The Chinese authorities should simply enforce all the traffic laws. Seat belt violations should be more than a $7.00 fine; drunk driving should carry more penalty than three days in jail; pedestrians should have the right of way like the published version of the Chinese road rules mandate; red lights and stop signs should not be optional. The Chinese traffic law is almost identical to American traffic law, with the exception that American traffic law is enforced, sometimes too vigorously like in Portland, Oregon where the police sometimes shoot first and ask questions later.

The best way to enforce any law in China is to squeeze the offender's wallet. This would provide more money to the city coffers to give the police a raise, give the everyday people financial incentive to be more careful drivers, and make them more likely to share the road. The same concept applies with litter. Chinese always pay attention when money is involved. There is no greater motivator than cold, hard cash. (Want to spice up a taxi ride? Tell your cabbie you'll give him a 25 percent tip – an extra couple dollars – if he can drive eight miles in rush hour traffic in fifteen minutes.) Besides, enforcing the laws using monetary penalties could just very well provide the desired cooling effect the leaders in Běijīng have been seeking for their overheating economy. It would at least give the local governments a revenue stream to pay off the debts they accumulated from the Chinese stimulus program during the Great Recession.

I once asked a Chinese friend why people didn't follow the traffic laws, or opted to walk on the dirt path in the grass next to the "keep off the grass" sign, or fish in a pond right next to the "no fishing" sign, and she replied with, *jìn zhū zhě chì, jìn mò zhě hēi* (近朱者赤，近墨者黑) which is a Chinese saying that translates into English as, "You will be good if you make good friend, you will be bad if you make a bad friend." In two words, this phrase could simply translate into "social momentum". Maybe the

people also know that there is no significant punishment or negative consequence for breaking the rules. And so goes the same with Chinese drivers. Once the Broken Windows Theory pushes the social momentum into a positive, constructive direction, more people will feel compelled to follow the law for the benefit of themselves and society as a whole rather than because it's the law. I met one Chinese woman in Dàlián who developed a case of Clean Obsessive-Compulsive Disorder only after she returned from her university studies in New Zealand. Once she realized how dirty the China she grew up in really was, she became conscious of it to the point where it influences her daily life. So, there seems to be some truth to both this old Chinese saying.

One day in June 2009 when I was in Portland, Oregon for a home leave, my doorbell woke me up from a jetlag-induced afternoon nap. It was a college student collecting signatures for the American Civil Liberties Union (ACLU). As soon as he finished his pitch, I deadpanned, "I've been living and working in China for the past two and a half years and I've become a big fan of the authoritarian government." Wide-eyed and speechless, he moved on to harass my neighbor. I'm also a big fan of the Declaration of Independence and U.S. Constitution, but there's a time and a place for everything. In 1776, the stars and stripes aligned and it was the right time and place for the Declaration of Independence; and the stars and stripes aligned once again in 1787 when the U.S. Constitution was ratified. The circumstances surrounding those events made the timing right. Ditto with the fall of the Berlin wall in 1989 and the end of the Soviet Union in 1991. Anyone who thinks China should give up authoritarian rule should visit Xi'an on October 2 of any year; visit a Chinese train station at the start of the Lunar New Year holiday; or fly the United Airlines route from San Francisco to Beijing.

Many people in the Western world never miss a chance to chastise the Chinese government about its lack of democracy. At this point in time, these protests are unwarranted because they're premature. Before they master the ballot box, the Chinese first need to master - without heavy police supervision - how to successfully navigate crosswalks, on ramps, one-way streets, and of course, those pesky traffic circles and roundabouts.

CHAPTER 29

THE BEST OF BOTH WORLDS

IN MARCH 2010, JUST BEFORE THE THREE-DAY CHINESE TOMB SWEEPING holiday weekend, I was sitting in a Dàlián Kāi Fā Qū watering hole in *Wǔ Cǎi Chéng* (五彩城 Five Color City), a defunct children's attraction that was reborn as an adult playground of bars, karaoke dens, restaurants, sex shops, massage parlors, and hourly hotel rooms. While sipping yet another drink from the umpteenth bottle of vodka I kept behind the bar, Vicky the Chinese bartender asked me if I had any travel plans for the weekend. I told her I was going to Hong Kong. "I still have my Hong Kong visa," Vicky beamed proudly. "But why do you need a visa to visit Hong Kong if it's part of China? You don't need a visa to visit Shànghǎi, do you?" I pressed. She paused for a moment, smiled, and then reprimanded me with, "Why do you always want to talk politics?" since it wasn't the first time I asked her these same questions. This also wasn't the first time, and probably won't be the last time that a Mainland Chinese citizen could not give me a complete answer to a seemingly simple question.

Prior to April 2010, the last time I was in Hong Kong was in 1998 when Queen Elizabeth II still had her mug on the money and I was in transit to Thailand to take advantage of a fire sale vacation thanks to the Asian Financial Crisis. I never made it out of the airport in 1998, but since my Chinese assignment was quickly coming to an end, it was high time I visited Hong Kong while I could make a long weekend of it. I flew from Dàlián to Shēnzhèn where I met up with a native Dàlián friend at the airport who then accompanied me to the Luō Hú (罗湖) border crossing and onto Hong Kong Island. "I like Hong Kong," said Yán while we were on the train to my hotel. "The people are nicer and friendlier than they are on the Mainland." She made a point to note that the screaming kids on the train were from the Mainland while those that were sitting quietly with their parents were Hong Kong natives.

Hong Kong, figuratively and literally, was a breath of fresh air from Mainland China. After flying in from the brown and grey wastelands of yet another endless Dàlián winter, the warm weather and tropical vegetation made the contrast between the Mainland and Hong Kong even more pronounced. But because I was surrounded by Chinese signs and ethnic Chinese people, I felt like I had traveled into a parallel universe. The Hong Kong weather was foggy and windy, but at least the wind didn't smell like coal smoke, rotting fish or a nearby makeshift toilet that doubled as local shrubbery. The narrow streets and the skyscrapers that cling to the steep hillsides are a testament that the Brits are island natives who could maximize the use of what little horizontal land was available. They essentially fit the whole city into a five-pound bag. The Central District of Hong Kong, home to high-end shopping, fine dining, and most of the city's five-star hotels, was densely packed, but it didn't feel that way. The sidewalks were relatively free of people, and even at their busiest they were still pretty empty of people, cars, bicycles, and whatever. The city streets were full like any other city, but they were quieter than on the Mainland, giving the impression that they were empty. The noisiest things on the streets were the sounds emanating from the crossing lights to assist the blind people. In four days, I might have heard a car horn no more than a few times; and cars always yielded to pedestrians. For a moment, I felt as though I was back in Portland, Oregon, or even in a quiet version of Chinatown in lower Manhattan that sprouted palm trees. Who said that nothing ever good comes from war? Then again, there's Texas, Arizona, and New Mexico.

But what Hong Kong lacked in noise and dirt, it made up for in signage reminding people how to behave. No Hawking, No Hocking, No Sitting, No Smoking, No Feeding the Wildlife, Do Not Release Domestic Pets, Wash Your Hands if You Touch Bird Shit (my wording, but same meaning), and Don't Stand on the Rocks, etc. What I didn't see anywhere in the city were the *wén míng* signs that litter the Mainland. What made these signs all the more interesting was that people obeyed them. I was spending an inordinate amount of time looking at all the signs. So much that they eventually became a huge distraction. At one point I thought I was back in the U.S. when I saw a sign at a Starbucks store that said, "Caution: Use By Children Should be Supervised" on the tray holding the plastic knives, forks, and spoons. People sometimes forget that Darwinism is a good thing and should be allowed to take over.

Hong Kong Park probably has the highest density of signs in the whole city. The drinking fountains in Hong Kong Park come with instructions on how to properly use them, and one had a stern warning stating that the fountain was "Just For Drinking Only." At first, one would think this most obvious, but it reminded me of a story an American coworker in Dàlián once told me: When he looked out onto the courtyard of his Dàlián apartment complex one morning, he saw a man approach a fountain, pull down his pants, wash his ass in the fountain, pull up his pants, and walk away.

After a couple days of Hong Kong, it was time to change up the scenery. With Macau only an hour away by TurboJet ferry (if you go, go SuperClass), it only made sense to go and see what the big deal was about. Having arrived in Macau at 2:30 p.m., I was a bit concerned that I wouldn't have enough time to appreciate the place before my 6:15 p.m. departure. As I started out from

THE BEST OF BOTH WORLDS

Macau harbor, I saw that Macau was Hong Kong's grubby little cousin. There wasn't much sparkle, buildings were dingier, and the diesel exhaust was more pronounced. Of course, the Portuguese had founded the colony 300 years prior to the British occupation of Hong Kong, so they had more time to perfect the worn-out look. The casinos dotted across the city gave it the seedy feel that matched its reputation.

It was in Macau where I found the answer to the question I always asked Vicky: imagine a quaint traditional Portuguese city square jammed packed with Chinese tourists. The Chinese had completely overrun the place to the point of parody. I found the crowds to be a real downer, but at least I came out of the ordeal with all my personal belongings sans the few dollars I left behind at one of the casinos. Talking with another coworker about my trip, he told me that he had his pocket picked twice on a single trip to Macau. The first time he lost 5,000 Hong Kong Dollars, or about $650; the second time he lost only an empty wallet since he stashed his money and credit cards elsewhere. Macao, like Hong Kong, also requires the Mainlanders to have a visa to enter, but a walk through town showed that they tend to be a little less choosy about how many they let in the door.

After visiting both Macao and Hong Kong, I think I finally understand why I cannot get a clear answer about Hong Kong from my Mainland Chinese friends. In the four days of my journey I accumulated eight passport stamps and two additional currencies even though, according to every Mainlander I talked with, I never left China. When I was in the Shēnzhèn Airport waiting to fly back to Dàlián, I left Hong Kong as confused as I entered it. Apparently I'm not the only one who is confused about Hong Kong's status. During a lunch with a few Western diplomats after my trip to Hong Kong, they told me that when Mainland Chinese citizens applying for visas to their country are asked, "have you ever been abroad" they would sometimes reply, "Yes, I've been to Hong Kong..." When I heard this, I couldn't help recall my days in Ireland in 1995-1996 when Mad Cow disease was all the rage and British beef was banned from export: all of a sudden the Unionist farmers in Northern Ireland claimed that they were actually raising *Irish* beef.

Not only are some Mainlanders confused about Hong Kong, some Hong Kong residents are in the same boat. According to his 2009 book, *Global Culture/Individual Identity: Searching for Home in the Cultural Supermarket*,[108] Gordon Matthews indicated that in a 1986 survey of Hong Kong residents, 59 percent thought of themselves as "Hongkongese" and 36 percent as "Chinese". By 1996 another survey showed that 35 percent considered themselves Hongkongese while 30 percent thought they were Chinese, and 28 percent classified themselves as Hong Kong Chinese. After Hong Kong was handed over to Běijīng in 1997, a survey

---

108 Matthews, Gordon, *Global Culture/Individual Identity: Searching for Home in the Cultural Supermarket*, Routledge, New York, New York, 2000.

showed that while 88 percent of Běijīng residents and 82 percent of Guǎngzhōu residents felt that those living in Hong Kong were Chinese, only 43 percent of those in Hong Kong who responded to the survey had any inclination toward a Chinese identity. Matthews also found that in October 1998, only 21 percent of the respondents in Hong Kong considered themselves Chinese.

It seems that the passage of time is only strengthening the identity of the Hong Kong people. In a December 2011 study by the University of Hong Kong,[109] only 17 percent of the Hong Kong citizens polled identified themselves as "Chinese citizens" (a 12-year low) while 38 percent of the respondents identified themselves as "Hong Kong citizens", a ten-year high. The study also showed that about 63 percent of the respondents identified themselves "in the broad sense" as "Hong Kong People", while about 34 percent identified themselves "in the broad sense" as "Chinese People." Making things even more confusing, about 43 percent of the respondents – an increase of 11 percent over the 2010 poll – identified themselves as a mixed identity of "Hong Kong citizens" plus "Chinese citizens."

To help everyone, including myself, with our confusion, conflicting clarity, or whatever one may want to call it about Hong Kong, I would like to propose a solution. First, there should be no debate that Hong Kong, Macau, and Mainland China are a single entity with no political boundaries separating the two. Second, the name of the political entity in its singular entirety shall be called, "The People's Republic of China". Hong Kong and Macau are part of China, end of story. Thirdly, consider pegging Hong Kong Dollar (HKD) and Macau Pataca (MO) to the Chinese RMB since the RMB has more value in U.S. dollar terms, and then eventually phase out the HKD and MO as the RMB transitions into a globally-traded currency, if, for anything, to remove the gaudy 10 HKD note – apparently printed with the ink that no

109 http://hkupop.hku.hk/english/release/release884.html

other country wanted – from circulation. Fourthly, convert any political boundaries into societal boundaries, and keep the visa requirements in place. Societal boundaries? The Customs officials will become social customs officials and not the political or taxing type. Fifthly, every few years or so depending on the progress seen from enforcing all the rules and creating a legal system based on the rule of law, expand the societal border separating Hong Kong, Macau, and the Mainland by a radius of about 100 miles to allow for the societal assimilation of all the people who live within the new radius. In about 50-100 years, China will be a peaceful, harmonious, civilized society with surplus *wén míng*. Hong Kong and Macau become part of China and China becomes part of Hong Kong and Macau. Implementing the best of both worlds becomes a win-win situation for all.

It took the Brits from the end of the First Opium War in 1842 to its 1997 handover to China to make Hong Kong into what it is today, and I'm confident that they didn't pull any punches during the early days when they were managing the territory. So, those responsible for Chinese unification have precedent on their side. The added bonus is that the Chinese government also has absolute authority and about $3 trillion in foreign reserves. What's the point of having a perfectly good authoritarian government and a shitload of cash if both are not put to good use? There's no doubt this next Cultural Revolution will be messy and difficult, but it won't end like the last one. It will be short term pain for long term gain for all of China. If done right the global balance of power will make a definitive shift to the east, and Vicky's grandchildren won't need to answer rhetorical questions from the likes of me.

CHAPTER 30

STRANGER IN MY HOMELAND

ABOUT TWO WEEKS BEFORE I WAS SCHEDULED TO REPATRIATE TO PORT-
land, Oregon, I was talking with an American coworker who had
been in China for just as long as I. Lin said to me, "it will probably
take about the same six months to adjust to living and working in
the U.S. as it did for us to adjust to living and working in China."
In some ways, I thought this a pretty fair statement, but since I
made a point to return to the U.S. a couple times each year during
my assignment, I thought six months was a bit too conservative.

It only took seconds after walking off the plane and into the
damp morning of May 3, 2010, to get used to the fresh air and blue
skies of Portland, Oregon. I was so keen on getting fresh air after
being cooped up in Chinese apartments for three and a half years
that I spent my entire first Sunday at home doing yard work. From
the moment I landed, I did what I could not do in Dàlián: sleep
with my bedroom windows open. Unfortunately, however, I was
awoken at 4 a.m. by a lonely bird looking for a playmate, which
was still much better than a car horn or a jackhammer. Now that
I no longer needed to work up the fortitude to enter a Carrefour
or any other grocery store, or spend a couple hours each weekend
on an Easter egg hunt to find all my groceries in stores scattered
across Dàlián, shopping became downright enjoyable since my

local New Seasons grocery store was just around the corner. Ditto for smoke-free fine dining; walking into a store and buying clothes and shoes that fit; fresh milk; an infinite number of beers with flavor; and the same number of wines at decent prices that I know will taste good. The highlight of my first week in Portland was spotting the waxing and shaving kits in the toiletries aisle of one local grocery store (not New Seasons, that's for sure) since many Chinese girls have yet to learn the concept of less being more.

In some respects – more than Americans would probably like to admit – some things haven't changed. Loogies still litter the sidewalks; I had to travel all the way to Chandler, Arizona in May 2012 to get t-boned at 40 mph by a white woman who didn't even acknowledge the existence of the red light she blew through; and spitters, pissers, and smokers still roam free, albeit in fewer numbers. Under American urinals, a yellow creek is more common than a yellow river. On a positive note, the black tights and short denim skirt look has made it to Portland even though it looks better on Asian girls. I saw two women walking arm-in-arm, which is common in China, but since this is Portland there's a good chance that they were more comrades than just friends. And to this day, I still have to remind myself every once in a while that staring at people is not culturally acceptable in the U.S.; and that a woman sitting alone at a bar, in a restaurant, or a hotel lobby isn't necessarily a hooker. I spotted one loud cell phone talker guy at an outdoor cafe that seemed to be in a huff about not wanting a diesel-powered car, "because," as he announced to the entire neighborhood, "I don't know how to drive a diesel!" I guess no one told him diesel cars drive the same as those which take gas. Dude, nut up and shut up. Then again, I was back in Portland, Oregon.

Besides all the friends I made, there are many other things I'm going to miss about China. Take, for example, the blatant disregard for the open container law and the drinks to go (which eliminates alcohol abuse); buying liquor by the bottle at the bar; inexpensive, market-fresh dining; tasty vegetables; walking out of a bar and not paying my bill until the next visit if I happened to be short of cash; harassing the wait staff in restaurants as I practiced my Chinese; the $6/week housekeeper; one-hour massages for $15; my driver; using my whiteness to my advantage; and no dropped mobile calls or dead zones even in the remotest countryside (AT&T could learn a few things from the Chinese). The one thing that I won't miss is not blending in. In Portland, being white gives me back my anonymity, and I'm perfectly okay with that.

On a deeper level, however, I know that I'll never fully repatriate. Not because I don't want to, but simply because I can't. There are just things that I can't, and will probably never, understand about American society, its odd set of priorities, and its myopic view or disregard for the rest of the world. For example, while watching the Animal Planet channel about training misbehaving dogs, there was an advertisement for Latisse,[110] a drug that will cure hypotrichosis, which is another word for having inadequate or not enough eyelashes. Honestly, do I need to say any more about this? Maybe this is my initiation back into the world of the mundane and petty after having traveled through places where the monthly household income is less than a happy-hour bar tab. Eyelashes? Really? Then again, as one American friend in Richmond, Virginia told me after my return, "bigger eyelashes and erections, that's what people care about." Mike was onto something because, shortly afterwards, I overheard a guy talking to two women in one of Portland's classiest wine bars about how he bumped into a 35-year-old retired porn star somewhere in his travels. One would think that there might be lower hanging fruit on the tree, such as the economy, the homeless, the quality of the public schools, and the national debt, but I guess not. Aren't we supposed to be suffering a hangover from the Great Recession? By the way, how many are "enough" eyelashes? Count yours up and let me know. All you Priapus wannabees can keep your

110 http://www.latisse.com/

erections to yourself, but don't forget to seek immediate medical attention if it lasts longer than four hours.

The American way of life just doesn't seem to get the blood flowing like a typical day in China. Gone is the continuous sensory bombardment – the sounds, sights, smells...oh, the smells – of a typical Chinese day. To the dismay of Guns N' Roses, China isn't a democracy, but it's a shining example of libertarianism at its best...and its worst: 1.34 billion people doing whatever 1.34 billion people want to do. If keeping an eye on all the people around you wasn't enough to keep the brain revved up, then there were the survival instincts that piled on top. Drinking tap water could land you in the hospital, and the Chinese did, after all, put the "M" in milk. Eating was always an adventure, and the thought, "will this get me sick?" preceded every first bite of any dish of food. When a group of us went to dinner in China we would be careful to never visit a new restaurant the night before anyone had to board an airplane. Then again, I've had food poisoning more times from eating company food service in Oregon than I've had in all my trips to China since 2003. Maybe I should be more careful of what I eat now that I'm back in the U.S.

And so should most Americans. Holy French Fries Batman, how did the whole country let itself go like it has? You know things are getting bad when ambulances need to reinforce their carriages to handle the added weight of heavy patients. Now I understand why one coworker in his 40s, who repatriated to the U.S. a year before I did, returned to his high school weight before returning to his normal weight: he refused to eat more than lettuce until he found a healthy balance. These days, I find myself eating just enough that I'm hungry about 30 minutes before the next meal. When I do eat, I tend to eat more fruits and vegetables and I'm more conscious of my caloric intake. Salads have become my friend. I've even consciously accepted an increased risk of spontaneous human combustion by upping my intake of shredded wheat now that I'm no longer paying $8.00 per box. After not eating all day during my first yard work excursion, I decided to go to my local burrito place that I visited weekly before I moved to China. Once I swallowed the last bite of what must have been a three-pound burrito, I felt like a python that swallowed a goat, and I didn't know which end I should let the burrito exit. Two days later, I felt as though I was still digesting it. I gained seven pounds in my first three weeks back in Portland; after a year of being back in Oregon, I was up almost 18 pounds and my blood pressure and cholesterol were on the rise. It just goes to show that American food is poisonous, and a Western diet just doesn't flow as well as a Chinese one. I guess I better go buy a couple more fire extinguishers and eat still more shredded wheat, or pick up a few bottles of Colon Flow ("As we discussed on TV, if you're not evacuating properly, you could be carrying pounds of extra weight!"[111]) or probiotic yoghurt to lighten my load. Could it be that people are trying to enhance their eyelashes and erections to compensate for all their other parts that are expanding out of control?

When I was in Ireland on a business trip in January 2010, I met up with one of my expat coworkers who repatriated six months before me. Alison said to me, "our China experience seems like a strange, distant dream." But if my time back in Portland has been any indication, China will never be too far away. At dinner on my first Saturday back in town, I met a guy who built the first 20-storey building in Dàlián in the 1980s, which was brought back to the ground in a blaze of dynamite in early 2011; a friend introduced me to an American woman in Portland who I first met by accident in late 2006 in a Shànghǎi wine bar; I started taking Mandarin lessons again; and I found a place where I can get authentic Chinese food without speaking a word of English. Someone must have heard about my return to Portland and wanted to ease my adjustment because at the four-way intersection in my neighborhood there are now brown people selling fresh fruit on the sidewalks.

111 http://www.colonflow.com

Those brown people aren't African-Americans, because the Portland Police tend to shoot and kill them. I guess some things just never change. On the bright side, no one should be too concerned about discrimination-fueled killings because the Portland Police also shot and killed a white homeless guy with a box cutter.

In a way, I think being back in Portland has magnified the culture shock. In China, I could always count on seeing people that were, on average, 5-foot-5 with straight black hair, similar complexion, and the same color eyes. It became comfortable, and interactions and situations became somewhat predictable. I saw the same thing every day. In Portland especially, it's clear that the U.S. is a nation of mutts; pink and green are not dyes but genetically-determined hair colors; and people come in all sorts of colors from a wide variety of cultures. In some respects it's not as predictable as China, and I can understand why my American coworker's Chinese wife, who immigrated to Portland in 2010, was at first a little skeptical about the people she encountered.

Since my return, I don't go out of my way to tell people that I went to China for a few years. Firstly, most people already have their minds made up about China; and secondly, they probably won't care, and I'm ok with that; and thirdly, no matter what I would say wouldn't even begin to do the experience justice. When I first repatriated, I went to see a well-produced, 86-minute, Emmy-nominated film called *Màn Zǒu* (慢走)[112] which means "Walk Slow", about four Americans from Seattle who bicycled from Běijīng to Shànghǎi in 28 days soon after the 2008 Summer Olympics. By chance, the team spent time in Dàlián while I was there in September 2008, but we never crossed paths. How does one boil down 28 days into 86 minutes? They did a fine job of capturing the feel of China, and had the advantage of video to tell their story, but they'll never be able to tell their whole story just like I won't be able to cover almost four years in a few minutes of

---

112 http://manzoumovie.com/

casual chit chat or this book. The only way for one to understand China is to experience it. Even though I'm wiser about China, I realize that I still don't truly understand it. I can say the same thing about the United States as well because now that I'm closing in on the three-year mark since my repatriation, I'm starting to think that Lin's estimate about a six-month adjustment might be more than just bit too light. I'm just glad that China taught me to be patient...

ACKNOWLEDGEMENTS

THERE IS ONLY ONE NAME ON THE COVER, BUT MAKING THIS BOOK A reality was hardly a singular effort. First of all, I'd like to thank a cast of characters who, while in China with me, were not only a source of inspiration but who made my Chinese adventure an incredible life experience: Jeremy Wikstrom, Darren Lombardi, Jack Mastrorilli, Todd Lasater, Richard Barwick, Allison Dineen, Rock Hardgrove, Joe Garside, Kris Lee, Kevin Judge, Izola Vaughn-Raysor, John Docherty, Paul Chen, Brian White, Jackie McConnell, Winny Que, Nair Maheswaran, Jon Gregg, Wayne Bunker, Anne (Town) Berry, Dave and Margot Fowles, and Gail Womack. Special thanks goes out to Jon Preston, because without his support I wouldn't have been a China expat in the first place. I would also like to thank all my Chinese friends who tolerated my curiosity and constant questioning; and who provided me their honest opinions, not knowing that what they told me would end up in print. For obvious reasons I won't mention them by name, but if they happen to read this book they will know who they are.

A big thanks goes out to Sean Jones at Inkwater Press for taking on this project; Masha Shubin at Inkwater for working her magic to turn a pile of text into a finished product; and to Ashley Goepfert for prepping the photos for publication. Also, without the creative inspiration of my childhood friend, Shane White (www. studiowhite.com), the cover design would not have been possible. As for the manuscript, I'm grateful for those who read some or all of it and provided their opinions, constructive feedback, and moral support along the way: Rob and Veronica Anderson, Lin Harris, Walden Kirsch, Rich McQueen, Barbara Haney, Brian Provencher, James Varnado, Randa McIntosh, Robert Shurtleff, Carol Strunk, David Medina, David Blackford, Jack Fulcher, Tod Ruckdeschel, Renato Reyta, Justin Robinson, Steve Hopkins, Jennifer "Gigi" McFadden, and author Marty Burkhart. A special thanks to Veronica Swehla, who, besides cutting my hair and reading through some chapters in her spare time even though I was just a shaggy walk-in off the street, provided the encouragement that helped to keep me motivated.

Last but most definitely not the least, I would like to thank my best friend and the love of my life, my amazing wife Reina, for all her patience, support, and dedication while I spent countless hours in front of the computer to finish this project. I can't imagine life without her, and I'm looking forward to plenty travel adventures with her by my side.

CPSIA information can be obtained at www.ICGtesting.com
Printed in the USA
BVOW010708071112

304909BV00006B/10/P

9 781592 998340